# A CHILD'S BIBLE

## *Lessons from the Torah*


*Seymour Rossel*



BEHRMAN HOUSE

# A CHILD'S BIBLE

## *Lessons from the Torah*

*Seymour Rossel*

BEHRMAN HOUSE

*Tanhuma teaches:*
Before God one righteous man is equal to the whole world,
as it is written,
"The righteous man is the foundation of the world" [Prov. 10:25].
This book is for **LEO H. TRAGER**
Without him, my world would have no foundation.
*S.R.*

---

**PROJECT EDITOR: RUBY G. STRAUSS**

---

**BOOK DESIGN: ROBERT J. O'DELL**

---

**STORY ILLUSTRATIONS: JOHN SANDFORD**
**EXERCISE ILLUSTRATIONS: JODY WHEELER**

**PHOTO CREDITS**
**Photo Researcher: R. Lynn Goldberg**

**6** Ira Block/The Image Bank; **11, 28, 43** (lower), **44, 99** (lower) United Nations Photo; **12** (upper), **19, 155** (lower) Four By Five; **12** (lower), **144** Courtesy, JNF; **27** (upper) Michal Heron/Monkmeyer; **36** A. B. Joyce/Photo Researchers; **43** (upper) Courtesy, NY Convention & Visitors Bureau; **67** (upper) Scott Ransom/Taurus Photos; **67** (lower) Charles Weckler/The Image Bank; **75** (upper) Sonya Jacobs/The Stock Market; **83** H. Armstrong Roberts; **92** Kahara/Peter Arnold Inc.; **99** Barbara Kreye/The Image Bank; **108** (upper) Grant Heilman; **127** Lenore Weber/Taurus Photos; **135** (upper) Bowman/H. Armstrong Roberts; **154** Porges/Peter Arnold Inc.; **160** Lee Boltin.

Through special arrangement with The Jerusalem Publishing House Ltd.: **20** (upper), **91** (upper) Azaria Alon; **35** (upper) Baruch Brendl; **59, 107** (lower), **108-9** (lower), **127** (upper), **135** (lower left), **145** (lower), **155** (upper) David Harris; **60** Palphot; **68** (upper) A. Hai; **75** (lower), **76** (lower) Nachum Slapak; **98** Israel Museum, Jerusalem; **100, 119, 136** Erich Lessing; **109** (upper) Israel Department of Antiquities and Museums; **118** (upper) A. van der Heyden; **119** (lower) Louvre, Paris; **135** (lower left) David Darom.

Photographs on pages **20** (lower), **27** (lower), **51, 52, 60** (upper), **68** (lower), **76** (upper), **84, 118** (lower), **145** (upper) are all subjects included in the Biblical Archaeology Slide Set of the Biblical Archaeology Society. Sets may be ordered by writing to 3000 Connecticut Ave. N.W. Suite 300 Washington, D.C. 20008.

Library of Congress Cataloging-in-Publication Data

Rossel, Seymour.
A child's Bible.

Contents: [1] Lessons from the Torah.
Summary: Stories from the Old Testament are accompanied by readings and activities for the Jewish Child.
1. Bible stories, English—O.T. Genesis. 2. Bible stories, English—O.T. Exodus. [1. Bible storie—O.T.]
I. Title.
BS551.2.R59 1987 222'.1109505 87-35070
ISBN 0-87441-466-0 (v. 1)

© COPYRIGHT 1988 BY SEYMOUR ROSSEL
**PUBLISHED BY BEHRMAN HOUSE, INC.**
Springfield, New Jersey

**ISBN 13: 978-0-87441-466-0**

MANUFACTURED IN THE UNITED STATES OF AMERICA

# CONTENTS

# INTROD

Time begins and ends–that is a Jewish idea. Before the beginning, there was God alone. At the end of days, God will remain. Our world is in-between.

We can never know what it was like before time began. And we can hardly imagine what it may be like when time comes to an end.

Some of our teachers say that our world is like a hallway. At the end of the hall a door opens to a wonderful dining room. Around the dinner table are all those who came before–Abraham, Sarah, Moses, Deborah–all your ancestors. Your job in the hallway, the teachers say, is to study and to do good deeds. Then you, too, will be ready to sit at the table. You, too, will be able to join in the great discussions of the wise.

But what shall we study? And how shall we know what deeds are good to do? Both questions have one answer: the *Torah*.

Our teachers saw people building, and saw how the builders first made a plan. As the builders worked, they checked their plan to be sure that the building would be a good one. Our teachers said, God worked in the same way. Before God began creating the world, God made a plan for the way the world should be. As God was creating, God checked to see if the world was "good." What was the plan that God used to build the world? It was the *Torah*.

The word *Torah* means "teachings." We sometimes use *Torah* to mean the first five books of the Bible: Genesis בְּרֵאשִׁית, Exodus שְׁמוֹת, Leviticus וַיִּקְרָא, Numbers בְּמִדְבַּר, and Deuteronomy דְּבָרִים. We also call these "The Five Books of Moses" חוּמָשׁ: *Chumash*). But sometimes we use *Torah* to mean the whole Bible and everything that we Jews have learned about the world.

# UCTION

Our teachers called the *Torah, Etz Hayyim,* "a tree of life." No doubt, they meant both the Five Books of Moses and all Jewish teaching.

God's commandments are a part of *Torah.* These instructions tell us how to live so that we will be good. Other parts of *Torah* are stories. The stories, too, are "teachings."

The stories tell us how people live, what people do, and how people behave. The people in the stories are always a lot like us. So the stories help us learn how we should live, what we should do, and how we should behave.

All the stories of the *Torah* are true. Yet this does not mean that the stories happened just as the *Torah* tells. When we talk about the *Torah,* we mean the stories are true in a different way.

The stories in our *Torah* are true because they teach us how to tell the difference between bad and good. So it does not matter if the world began in seven days or if it really took millions of years. The *Torah* story about how God created the world is still true. It is true because it teaches us that we are made "in the image of God." And it is true because it teaches us that resting on the Sabbath is good.

As you read the stories you should ask, "What truth is this story teaching me?" "What does this story say that I should do?" "How does this story say that I should behave?"

This book is made up of stories from the Bible. It is about the laws and the stories of the Jewish people, our *Torah.* Together, we will look at the teachings to see what they mean to us today. Along the way you may learn another thing, too. You may learn why our teachers call the *Torah* "a tree of life."

Genesis 1:1-2:4 בְּרֵאשִׁית

*Chapter 1*

# IN THE BEGINNING

In the beginning, God created the heaven and the earth.

God said, "Let there be light." And there was light. This light made the world bright from one end to the other.

God saw that the light was good, so God separated light from dark. God called the light Day, and God called the dark Night. The first evening came and the first morning followed. That was the first day.

Then God said, "Let there be space between the waters above and the waters below." And God called the space Sky. Evening came and morning came. That was the second day.

Then God said, "Let the waters below the Sky come together. Between the waters there will be dry land." God called the land Earth, and God called the waters Seas. And God saw that this was good.

God said, "Let plants and fruit trees grow up out of the Earth." And God saw that this was good. Evening came and morning came. That was the third day.

Then God said, "Let there be lights in the Sky." So God made the golden sun to shine by day, and the silver moon and stars to shine by night. And God saw that this was good. Evening came and morning came. That was the fourth day.

Then God said, "Let the waters fill to the brim with living things, and let birds fly across the sky." God created the great sea animals, and all the things that creep, and all kinds of birds. And God saw that this was good. God blessed all the living things, saying, "Have many children to fill the seas and the skies." Evening came and morning came. That was the fifth day.

Then God said, "Let the earth have every kind of living thing—cattle, small animals, and wild beasts." And animals came to life. There were tiny lizards and mammoth elephants and giant tigers. Later came horses and deer and wild mountain goats. And God saw that this was good.

Then God said, "Let Us make a person in God's image." And God created a person in the image of God. Male and female, God created people. God blessed them and said, "Have many children. Fill the Earth and tell it what to do. Rule over the fish, the birds, and all the living things."

God said to the people, "Look. I give you every plant and fruit tree. They shall be your food. And to the animals and birds I give all the green plants to eat." And so it was. God saw all that God had made, and found it very good. Evening came and morning came. That was the sixth day.

The heaven and the earth were finished and full of life. On the seventh day, God did not work. God rested.

God blessed the seventh day—the Sabbath day—and called it holy, because on that day God rested from the work of creating. And that is how Heaven and Earth were made.

WHAT DOES IT MEAN?

## "It is not good for people to be alone..."

God wants us to live, play, and work with other people. That is why God gave Adam a partner. Being alone is hard. Think of cleaning up your room. It always seems like such a big chore when you have to do it by yourself. But when someone else helps you, even cleaning up can seem like a game.

Taking care of the world is like that, too. God commanded us to rule over the world and care for it, to make it a better place to live. That is too big a task for any one person to do alone. But, if we work together, all as one, we can do even this giant chore.

WHAT DOES IT TEACH?

## A Special Garden

The Garden of Eden was a garden of trees. Sometimes we forget how much we need trees. Trees give us fruit and nuts and shade when the sun is hot. From wood we make paper, cardboard, and formica. Trees take in the air that is bad for us, and turn it into air that is healthy for us.

We celebrate the goodness of trees on *Tu B'Shevat,* the New Year of the Trees. This holiday comes as spring begins in the Land of Israel. In Israel *Tu B'Shevat* is a time for planting. We celebrate by singing and dancing.

**Working together we can do things that none of us can do alone.**

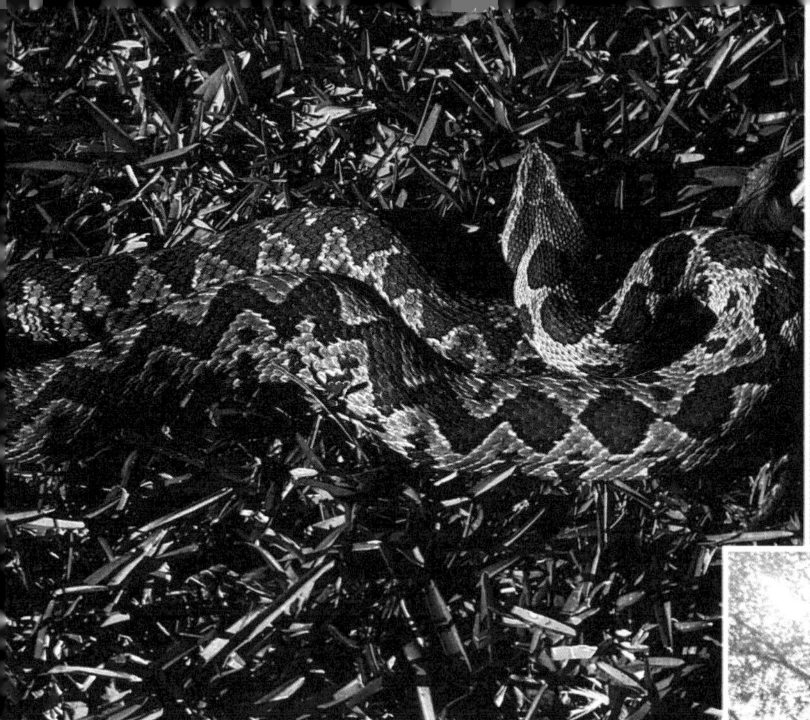

**As a punishment for tricking Eve, God cursed the snake and forced it to slither along on its belly.**

**Olive trees live hundreds, even thousands, of years, giving us precious gifts of fruit, oil, and wood.**

A LESSON ABOUT THE TORAH

## A Strange Snake Indeed

The Torah says that the snake in the Garden was smarter than all the animals.

Being smart is a gift from God. We can use that gift for doing good or for doing bad. Sad to say, the serpent spent all his time thinking up evil things to do.

But the woman still did not know about evil. When they came to the tree of knowledge, the woman told the serpent, "God said, 'Do not eat of it, or touch it, else you will die.'"

Really, God had only said, "Do not eat its fruit." God never told Adam not to touch the tree. That gave the serpent an idea.

Our teachers say: The serpent pushed Eve against the tree. He said, "Look, you touched the tree and you did not die. Now you can eat the fruit, too."

And that is how the serpent tricked the woman.

[Source: Gen. R. 19:3]

Find your way through the Garden of Eden.

# CROSSWORD PUZZLE

What filled the Garden?

To find out, fill in the words across. Then read your answer in the grey boxes.

1. One of the trees in the center of the Garden was the Tree of______________.

2. The other tree was the tree of______________.

3. Adam's partner was______________.

4. The Garden was in a place called______________.

The Garden of Eden was filled with______________.

---

# MYSTERY WORD

______________________________

is the New Year of the Trees.

# NAME THE ANIMALS

God brought all the animals to Adam.
Whatever Adam called each one,
that became its name.

Can you guess what Adam called these animals?

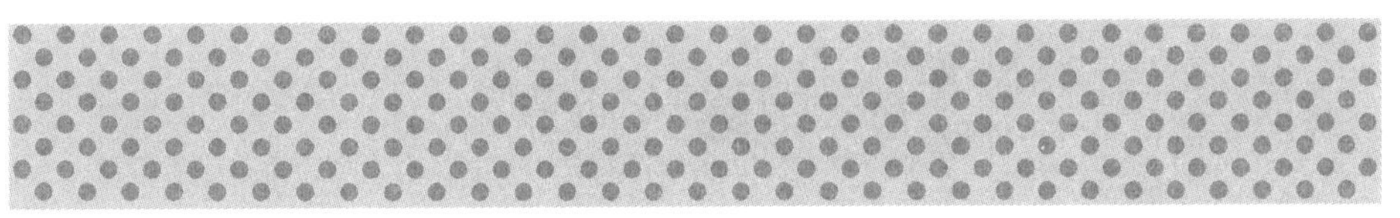

## Do you know why?

God made a partner for Adam because

The man and the woman hid from God because

God punished the snake because

God sent Adam and Eve out of the Garden of Eden because

*Chapter 3*

# THE TERRIBLE CRIME

dam and Eve learned to hoe the earth and plant seeds. They were farmers and they worked hard from sunup to sundown. God helped them and soon they had their first child. Eve called her first son Cain. Then Eve gave birth to his brother, Abel.

Abel became a shepherd, watching over goats and sheep. Cain became a farmer, planting and harvesting.

One day, Cain brought a gift to God from his farm. And Abel brought God the best of his newborn sheep. God smiled on Abel and his gift, but paid no attention to Cain. Cain was upset and sad.

God said to Cain, "Why are you upset, and why are you sad? Surely, if you do good things, you will feel good. But if you do bad things, evil will always be with you. Evil will lead you to do more evil. Only you can stop yourself from doing bad things."



But Cain was angry. He did not pay close attention to what God said.

One day Cain and Abel were in the field together. Suddenly, all of Cain's anger came out. He had a terrible argument with his brother Abel. In one awful moment, Cain attacked Abel and killed him.

God said to Cain, "Where is your brother Abel?"

Cain answered, "I do not know. Am I my brother's keeper?"

"What have you done?" God asked. "Listen! Your brother's blood cries out to Me from the ground! Now you will be more cursed than the ground! If you try to be a farmer, the ground will give you nothing. You will wander forever on the earth."

Suddenly, Cain was very sorry for what he had done. "My punishment is too great!" he said. "You forbid me to farm. You force me to wander, and not to see You. Now anyone who meets me might kill me!"

God said, "If anyone kills Cain, I promise to punish that person seven times over." And God put a mark on Cain, so that anyone who met Cain would know not to harm him.

Then Cain went away from God to live in the Land of Nod, east of Eden.

Adam and Eve had another child. Eve called him Seth. Time passed and Seth had a son named Enosh. It was in the time of Enosh that people began to pray to God.

WHAT DOES IT MEAN?

## And Eve gave birth to Cain.

The story of Cain and Abel is the story of the first children, the first family, the first prayer-sacrifice, the first jealousy, the first death, and the first murder—all in one.

The clue to what went wrong is in Cain's name. The name Cain means "I got." Cain was a person who loved getting, but not giving.

When the time came to give a gift to God, Abel brought the best of his sheep. He was generous. But Cain brought "a gift from the farm." It was something less than the best. He kept the best for himself.

Being selfish is not a crime. But it is not pleasing, either. People do not like sharing with or being with a selfish person. And, in the end, the selfish person not only hurts others, but is also hurt in return. That is the lesson Cain learned.

**Being selfish is not a crime, but it is not pleasing either.**

**A modern Arab farms just as Cain did, throwing seed by hand.**

**This Arab shepherd is proud of his best lamb, as Abel was when he chose the best animal to sacrifice to God.**

WHAT DOES IT TEACH?

## Punishing and Loving

After Abel died, Cain was sorry for what he had done. Even so, God had to punish Cain. If a person hurts another person, there must be a punishment. Cain's punishment was to wander, and never to have a home of his own. Being punished is one way we learn right from wrong.

But God loved Cain, too. That is why God told Cain to stop himself from doing bad. That is why God was angry when Cain killed Abel. And that is why God gave Cain a mark to protect him.

There are times when parents must punish us to teach us an important lesson. Part of that lesson is that a punishment made out of love can protect us and help us grow.

A LESSON ABOUT THE TORAH

## A Field of Strawberries

God said to Cain, "Where is your brother Abel?" Cain answered, "I do not know. Am I my brother's keeper?"

Our teachers say: This reminds us of a story. Once a person went into a field of strawberries. He took strawberries by the handful. He ate them. But the owner of the field came along and ran after this stranger. The owner said to the stranger, "What do you have in your hand?" The stranger said, "Nothing." The owner said, "Oh, no? Look! Your hands are red from the juice of the strawberries!"

It was the same with Cain's answer to God. God said, "Listen! Your brother's blood cries out to Me from the ground."

In the end, lies do not help us. Nearly always, the truth comes out.

[Source: Gen. R. 22:9]

# MULTIPLE CHOICE

Circle the word that best completes the sentence.

1. Cain and Abel were____________.
   **brothers cousins friends**
2. The name Cain means____________.
   **love stick I got**
3. Abel was a____________.
   **builder farmer shepherd**
4. God punished Cain because he killed____________.
   **sheep Abel Adam**
5. Cain was angry because God did not like his____________.
   **mark brother gift**
6. God put a mark on Cain so that no one would____________.
   **speak to him like him harm him**

---

# Be A Detective

God knew the terrible thing that Cain had done.

And the farmer knew that the stranger had eaten the strawberries.

How do you know when someone has done something wrong?

Connect the picture to show how you know.

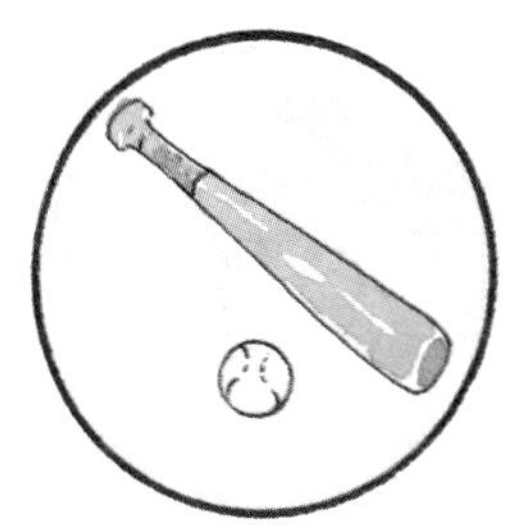

# YOU BE THE TEACHER

The story of Cain and Abel has many lessons to teach us.

Choose one of the lessons below and tell what it means to you.

**1**

The selfish person hurts others, but is also hurt in return.

**2**

If a person hurts another person, there must be a punishment.

**3**

If you do good things, you will feel good.

## *A Gift from God*

In the days of Cain and Abel, people brought animals and food to God as gifts. These gifts were called sacrifices.

Today we know that God wants different kinds of gifts. God wants us to share and not to be selfish. God wants us to love and not to hate. God wants us to care for other people and not to be mean.

Draw a picture or write about the kind of gift you can bring to God.

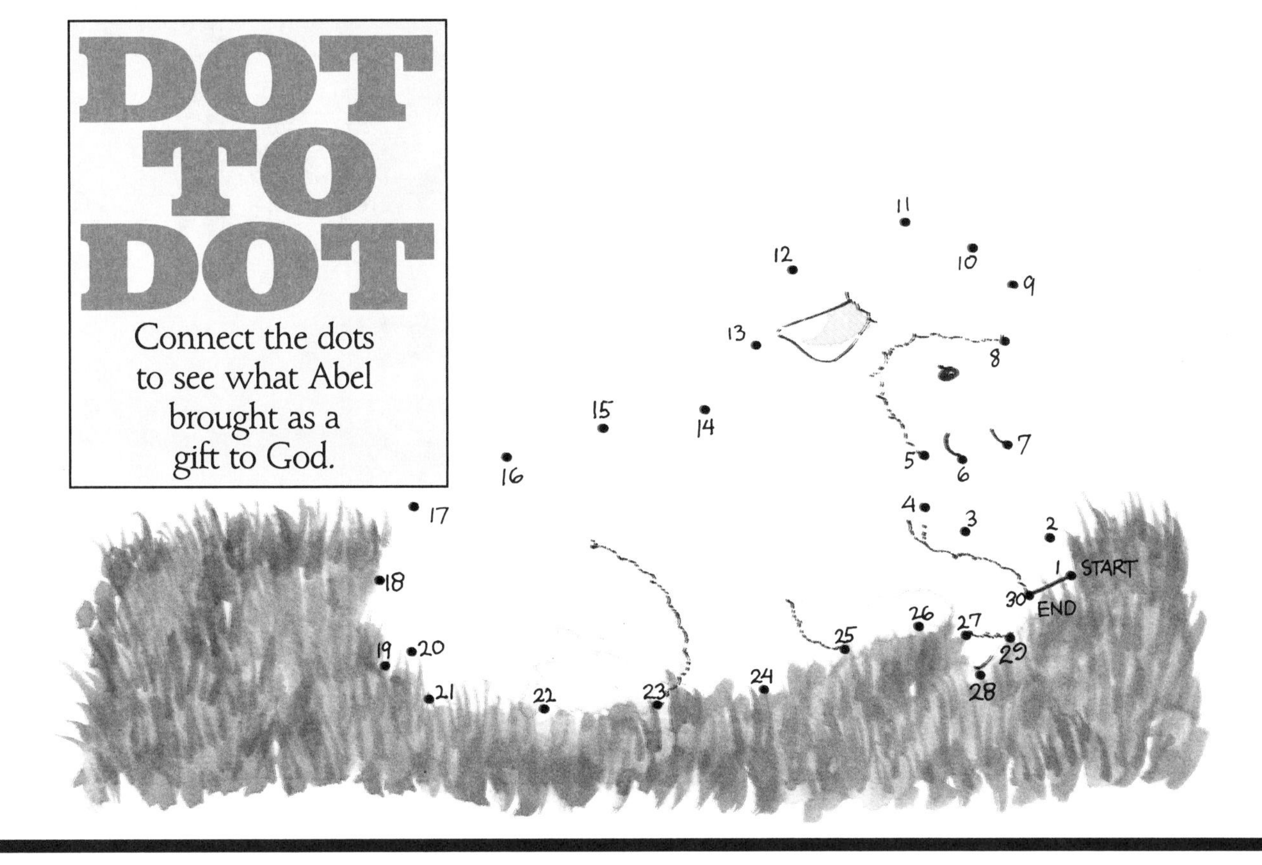


## MYSTERY WORD

Cross out any letter that appears two times.

| B | E | G | J | C | L | H |
|---|---|---|---|---|---|---|
| D | M | A | B | S | G | K |
| H | K | M | U | D | O | C |

Write the letters that are left here:

_____ _____ _____ _____ _____ _____ _____

Now unscramble the letters to see how Cain felt.

When we are ______________ we can make awful mistakes.

Genesis 6:5-9:17 בְּרֵאשִׁית

*Chapter 4*

# NOAH AND THE FLOOD

A time came when evil spread over all the earth. People did wicked things and God was sorry for creating them. God was sad. And God decided to wipe all the living things off the earth.

But Noah pleased God. In those days of wickedness, Noah was a good person. Noah walked with God.

God said to Noah, "I have decided to destroy all living things. Make an ark with many rooms and put a window in its top and a door in its side. And make it three stories high."



God said, "Soon I will bring the Flood: Waters will cover the earth and all the living things on earth will die. But I will make a covenant with you and your family. Two of every living thing will come to your ark to stay alive with you. Take all the food you will need, for you and for them, and store it away."

And Noah did everything just as God commanded.

When the ark was finished, God said, "You and all your family must go into the ark. Seven days from now, I will make it rain."

Noah and his family went aboard the ark. Animals and birds and insects–two of each, male and female–came to Noah's ark. For many days they came. Every kind of living thing came–from antelopes to zebras, from alligators to worms, even the giraffes, the hippos, and the bears.

On the seventh day, the Flood began. The earth shook and cracked, and water rushed up from every spring and well. The windows of the sky broke open, and rain poured down like waterfalls from heaven. God closed the ark up tight.

For forty days the flood waters rose, taking the ark higher and higher. The tops of the highest mountains were covered. Every breathing thing on the land was trapped in the water and died. Only Noah and those in the ark were left alive.

One hundred and fifty days passed. God did not forget Noah and the ark. At last, the rain stopped falling. At last, the waters were quiet.

And the ark came to rest on the mountains of Ararat. Slowly the water drained until the tops of the mountains could be seen.

Noah opened the window and sent out a raven. The heavy black bird flew and flew, searching for a place to land. Then Noah sent out a dove. But even the small white bird could find no place to rest. The dove returned. Noah put out his hand and took it into the ark.

He waited seven days. Again he sent out the dove. This time it came back at evening. In its beak was a leaf freshly torn from an olive tree. So Noah knew the earth was almost dry.

He waited seven more days. He sent the dove out again and when it did not come back, Noah knew the dove had found a place to land. Noah opened the ark.

Noah came out with all his family. The birds and the beasts and every living thing came out. It took a long time. Many baby animals had been born on the ark.

God blessed Noah and his family, and God made a covenant with Noah. God said, "Have children and fill the earth. Eat animals and grains. But do not eat animals that are still alive. And do not kill people. Because God made people in the image of God."

Suddenly the sun broke through the clouds to warm the earth. And in its light, a rainbow appeared, its colors flashing across the heavens.

God said to Noah and his family, "My rainbow will be the sign of the covenant between Me and you forever. Never again will there be a flood to destroy the earth."

Mount Ararat in eastern Turkey: The Bible tells us that the Ark came to rest on the top of this mountain after the Flood.

WHAT DOES IT MEAN?

## Noah walked with God.

Walking with God means following God's laws and commandments. It means behaving in the ways that God shows us. The people who died in the flood were wicked. They did not walk with God, so God destroyed them.

But God doesn't tell us how to behave all the time. God wants us to learn right from wrong by studying the world around us.

Our teachers say: First God created the Torah and all its laws. Then God created the world using the laws of the Torah. When we study the Torah, we are studying the same laws that God built into our world. It is the Torah which teaches us how to walk with God.

Every mezuzah is a symbol. This silver mezuzah was made in Russia nearly one hundred years ago. What does the symbol of the mezuzah help us remember?

**Every rainbow can be a symbol reminding us of God's promise to Noah. It is up to us to remember its meaning.**

WHAT DOES IT TEACH?

## The Lesson of the Rainbow

God created the rainbow long before the time of Noah. The rainbow is part of nature. It appears when sunlight strikes a misty sky in a certain way. God simply told Noah to remember the covenant whenever he saw a rainbow.

Something that helps us remember another thing is called a "sign" or a "symbol." When we see the sign on the corner that says "walk" or "wait," it reminds us that there is a right time to cross the street.

A mezuzah is a sign, too. As we leave our house, and when we return home, seeing a mezuzah on the doorpost reminds us that we should follow God's commands everywhere we go.

Whenever you see a rainbow, remember the story of the Flood and God's promise that never again would a Flood cover the whole earth.

A LESSON ABOUT THE TORAH

## Why Noah Built the Ark

God could have found many ways to save Noah from the Flood. Just by speaking, God could have saved him.

Our teachers say: God told Noah to build the ark because God knew that building an ark would take lots of time and work.

Noah's neighbors would gather around and say, "What are you making?"

Noah would say, "An ark. Soon God will bring a Flood to destroy the earth."

In this way, Noah's neighbors would have plenty of time to change their ways. They could do good instead of bad. And, if God saw them doing good, then God would not have to destroy the world after all.

That is what God wanted. But the people were very wicked. They paid no attention to Noah at all.

[Source: Tanhuma]

# SYMBOLS

A thing that helps us remember something else is called a "symbol."
What do these symbols help you remember?

## Looking For Understanding

1. Why did God decide to send the Flood?
2. Why did God save Noah?
3. Why did God tell Noah to build an ark?
4. Who went into the ark with Noah?
5. Why did Noah send a raven and a dove out of the ark?
6. When we see a rainbow what do we remember?
7. What does it mean to "Walk with God"?

LETTER

VVVV

OOOO

CCCC

## NAME SCRAMBLE

Unscramble the letters to see the names of people you know.

VEE____________________

AMDA____________________

NAIC____________________

LBAE____________________

NHOA____________________

# SCRAMBLE

AAAA TTTT NNNN NNNN EEEE

There are 8 letters
in the rainbow.
Write them here _ _ _ _ _ _ _ _
Write the letters in the correct order.

God made a __________
with Noah.

# WHAT IS THE MEANING?

Write each word next to its meaning.

**FLOOD ARK RAINBOW DOVE**
**RAVEN COVENANT MEZUZAH SYMBOL**

| | DEFINITIONS |
|---|---|
| | much water all at once |
| | what Noah built |
| | colors in the sky |
| | a small white bird |
| | a large black bird |
| | an agreement we promise to follow |
| | what we put on our doorpost |
| | a thing that reminds us of something else |

*Chapter 5*

# A TOWER TO THE SKY

n those days everyone on earth spoke the same language. They called things by the same names. And all together, they wandered as one tribe, living and speaking as one people.

Once they came to a green and rolling valley in the land called Shinar. It was there they decided to stay.

They said, "Come, let us take clay from the ground and use it to make bricks. We will bake the bricks to make them hard."

So they made bricks into stones for building, using tar to hold the stones together.

They decided to build a mighty city and a tower of brick. "We will make the tower so tall it will touch the clouds in the sky," they said. "People will then remember us and praise our name. People will want to live in our city forever."

For many years they built. As time passed, more and more people came to join them. It seemed that all the people of the earth were gathering together in one place. The people thought, "Together, we are very great. Together, we can do what only God could do before."

God saw the bricks becoming a city and a tower. God watched as the hearts of the people became as hard as bricks. The people of the earth stopped loving one another. They forgot how to love God. No more did they stop to look at the flowers growing on the hillsides. No more did they pause to watch the splendor of a sunset. They cared only about building the tower and the city.

The tower was raised brick by brick. As it grew higher, the workers looked down on the people in the city below. The people below looked as tiny as ants. It made the builders feel mighty and strong. "We can build our tower into heaven itself," they said. "We can make war with God."

So God decided to teach them a lesson. God said, "When they talk, let them babble like the noise of water rushing over bricks. They will not understand each other. Then their building, and their evil, will come to an end."

God made their language into many languages. People wondered why no one could understand them. The making of bricks stopped. People argued and did not know what their arguing was all about. The building stopped.

People gathered together into small tribes that spoke one language. They said, "Let us leave this place and make a home together somewhere beyond these hills."

The city was never finished, and the tower never reached the clouds. People set out for places all around the earth.

So, from that time to this, people call that place Babel, because in Babel God babbled the language of the whole earth.

WHAT DOES IT MEAN?

## "We can make war with God."

The builders on the tower looked down and saw everything below getting smaller and smaller. It made them feel stronger and more important than the people below. They began to think that they were as mighty as God.

You do not have to be on top of a tall tower to look down on other people. You can just say or think that a person is someone to "look down on," someone less important than you.

But, really, God makes each of us special, so every person is important. Every person has something special to offer the world. "Looking down" on people is always a mistake. It's like "making war with God."

**The Empire State Building: One of the most famous skyscrapers in the world. Can you imagine how the people of the city below looked to the workers who built this modern-day ziggurat?**

**At the United Nations people speak many languages, but try hard to understand one another so that the nations of the world can live together in peace.**

**God made each of us special and different. It is up to us to learn how to share one world, making it better for all.**

WHAT DOES IT TEACH?

## A Tower to the Sky

The tower in the story was a kind of pyramid called a *ziggurat.* Almost always, the reason for building it was to worship a false god at the top. The builders wanted the people below to worship them the way we worship God. They knew no tower could really reach the sky. But the builders wanted their tower to be the highest in the world. Then other people might think the builders were the greatest and mightiest people in the world and want to be just like them.

But God does not want us all to be alike. God did not give us one face, one color of skin, or one way of thinking. God wants each of us to be special. So God divided these people and sent them to all corners of the earth.

It is wrong to think that all humans should be one and the same. In truth, God is One and Unique, while we are many and different.

A LESSON ABOUT THE TORAH

## What Is Really Important?

Our teachers say: The Tower of Babel had seven steps from the east and seven steps from the west. On one side they brought up huge bricks. On the other side people went down again. As the tower grew taller, it took many years to bring a brick to the top. So it seemed that the bricks were more important than people.

If a person fell off the tower, people did not even stop working. They paid no attention at all. But if one brick fell down, they would sit and weep. They would cry, "Woe to us! When will another brick be brought up to replace the one that fell?"

God wants us to remember what is really important. Bricks can never be more important than life. Things are never as important as people. That is what the builders forgot, and that is what we must always remember.

[Source: Pirke deRebbe Eliezer]

# MAZE

God divided the people
and sent them to all
corners of the earth.
Help them find their way.

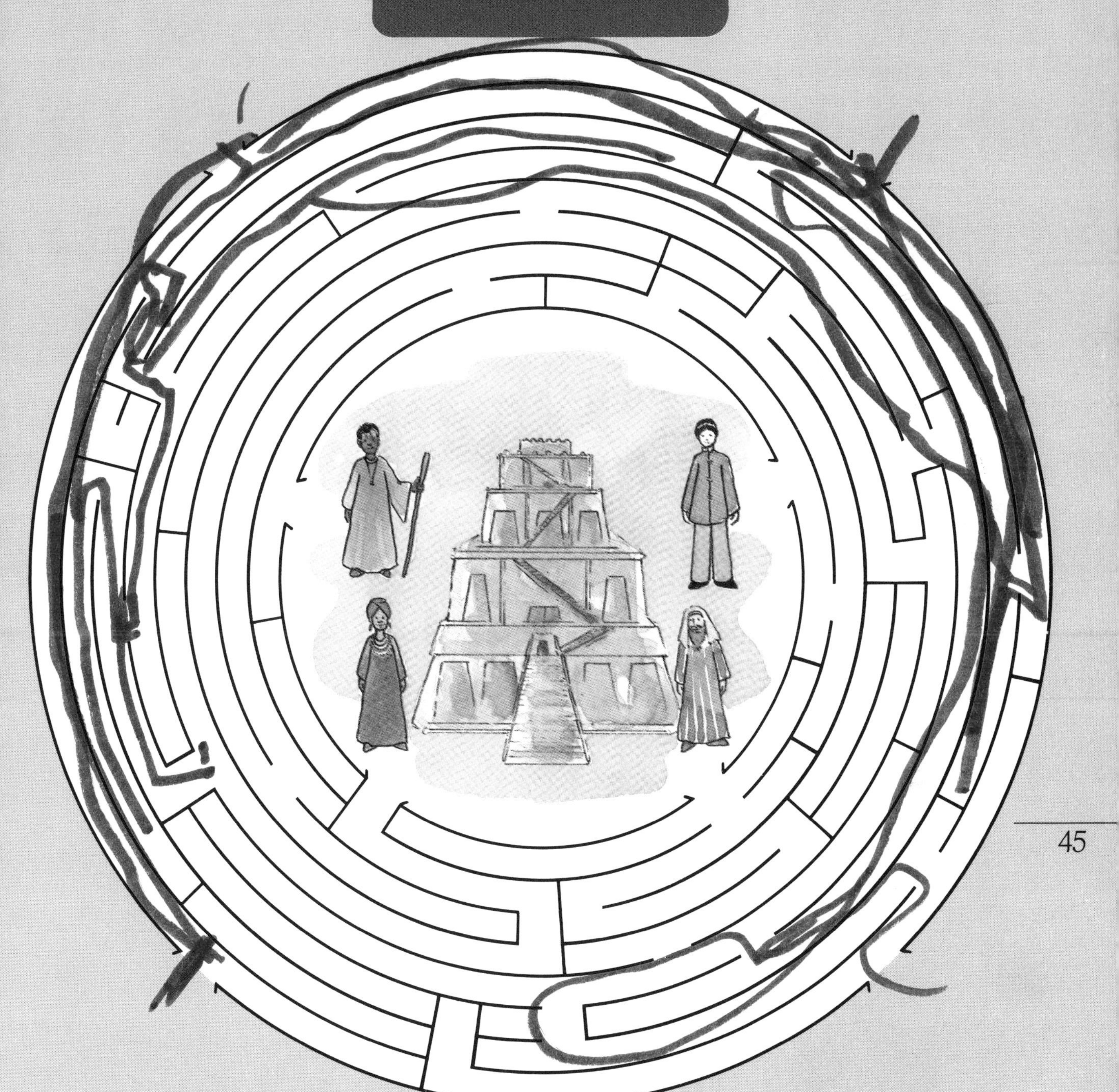

## You Be The Teacher

The story about the tower of Babel has many lessons to teach us. Choose one of the lessons below and explain what it means to you.

1. "Looking down" on people is always a mistake.
2. God wants each of us to be special.
3. Every person has something special to offer the world.
4. Things are never as important as people.

## DO YOU KNOW WHY?

The people decided to build a tall tower because

______________________

The people stopped loving one another because

______________________

The builders felt mighty and strong because

______________________

The people left the place because

______________________

The place is called Babel because

______________________

## WORD SCRAMBLE

Put the letters in each brick in the correct order. Can you use the words to tell a story about the tower of Babel?

SRB KCI ______________

BLB EBA ______________

WET RO ______________

DBI UL ______________

YCI T ______________

ITM HGY ______________

# PICTURE MESSAGE

Can you read the message below?

The 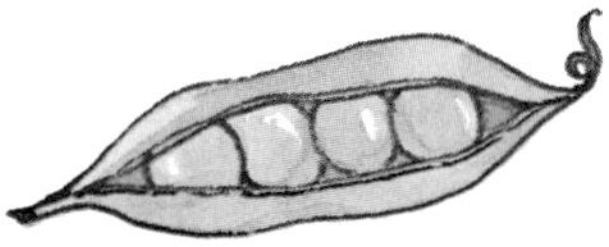 ple D cided

2 B  d A Ci

tall it  reach

the  T

4 got W  was 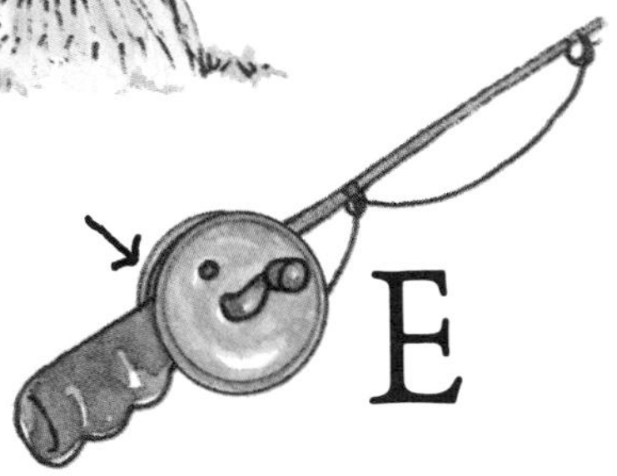 E

import

Write the message here.

*Chapter 6*

# ABRAM WALKS WITH GOD

n the city of Haran, lived Abram and his wife Sarai. They had no children. Then Abram's brother had a child named Lot. Abram and Sarai treated their nephew Lot just like a son.

One day, God said to Abram, "Leave your homeland and your father's house. Go to the land I will show you. You will be the father and Sarai will be the mother of a great nation. Your name will be remembered."

Abram, Sarai, and Lot packed up all they owned. They loaded their donkeys and set out on the road. The days of travel were long, but at last they came to the Land of Canaan.

At first, Abram and Lot had little. When they made camp together beside a well, there was plenty of water and plenty of room. Abram and Lot worked hard and in time they grew rich. Abram's riches were cattle, silver, and gold. Lot's riches were flocks of goats and sheep, and herds of cattle. Now when they made camp together, they were too many in one place. The workers who took care of Abram's cattle began to argue with the workers who took care of Lot's animals. It seemed there was never enough water and never enough grass.

One day, Abram took Lot out to the edge of a cliff. Abram said to Lot, "We are one family. My workers and your workers must not argue. You and I must live in peace. Look around. The land is wide and every part of it is blessed by God. Choose what pleases you. If you go north, I will go south. If you go south, I will go north."

Lot knew that Abram was right. He looked around. Near the city of Sodom, the land was green and full of trees. Lot thought, "There is a place like the Garden of Eden." He saw the Jordan river winding through the open fields. Lot thought, "There is a river like the great Nile of Egypt."

Then Abram hugged his nephew. They promised to remember each other always. With tears in their eyes, they parted. Abram stayed in the Land of Canaan, while Lot set up his tents near Sodom.

God spoke to Abram again. God said, "You have done what is good and what is fair. Now, look up and look around. I will make your family like the dust that covers the earth. And no one can count the dust of the earth. Rise up and walk through all the land."

God said, "This land will belong to you, your children, and the children of your family forever."

WHAT DOES IT MEAN?

## "Leave your homeland..."

Growing up means making many choices. And the choices you make depend on the kind of person you are, the kind of family you have, and the kind of friends and neighbors around you. God told Abram to leave his friends and his father's house for a good reason.

Abram grew up in the cities of Ur and Haran. These cities were full of idol worshipers. An idol is a statue. It is supposed to look like one of the many gods. In olden times, people offered prayers and sacrifices to idols, hoping the gods would help them.

Abram's friends worshiped idols. And our teachers say that Abram's father was a maker of idols. In time, Abram might turn to the ways of his friends. He might worship idols and forget the One God.

In time, we grow to be more and more like our friends. So learning to choose the right friends is an important part of growing up.

**Doll-sized idols like these were called "household idols." Abram's father may have made idols like these, or the huge statue-sized idols that stood in temples.**

**Together, Abram and Lot had so many sheep that their herds could not live close together in peace.**

WHAT DOES IT TEACH?

## Peace at Home

Abram said to Lot, "There must not be arguments between you and me... We are family." This is the Jewish idea of *shalom bayit.* It means "peace at home." Before there can be peace in the world, we must first learn to live peacefully with people who are close to us. We must learn to live in peace with our parents and grandparents, brothers and sisters, uncles and aunts, and cousins.

Sometimes, to live at peace we have to give up more than seems fair. Abram asked Lot to choose whatever part of the land Lot wanted. Lot chose what looked like the best part. But Abram did not complain. Even if Lot took more than what was fair, Abram knew it was worth giving a little more to gain *shalom bayit.*

Sometimes parents ask us to do more than we think is fair. Or a brother or sister may borrow or take something that is important to us. That is the time to remember the idea of *shalom bayit.* Learning to give a little more can often bring peace at home. And learning to bring peace at home can help us learn how to bring peace to the world.

A LESSON ABOUT THE TORAH

## Why Should We Be Like the Dust of the Earth?

God said to Abraham, "I will make your family like the dust that covers the earth." Our teachers say: There are many ideas in this one. Here are three:

(1) As dust rubs against things, it scratches at them like sandpaper. Dust can wear away even the strongest iron. In the same way, the Jewish people can wear away all evil ideas. We can lead many nations to God.
(2) Dust covers all the earth. So, too, the Jewish people live throughout the world.
(3) There are so many specks of dust on the earth that no one can count them. So the Jewish people one day will be too many to count.

[Source: Yalkut Me'am Lo'Ez]

# SEPARATE THE FLOCKS

Abram is going to stay in the Land of Canaan. Lot will set up his tents near Sodom. Help them separate their animals. Mark the cattle with an A. Mark the sheep and goats with an L.

## TEST YOURSELF

Circle the correct word to complete each sentence.

1. On the seventh day God created (REST THE SUN SEA MONSTERS).
2. God made people in God's (TIME OVEN IMAGE).
3. God said, "It is not good for people to be (TOGETHER ALONE GREEN).
4. God sent Adam and Eve out of the Garden of Eden to (FARM OWN SPOIL) the land.
5. Cain asked God, "Am I my brother's (BARBER SEEKER KEEPER)?
6. Noah was good in his time. He (WALKED PRAYED SAILED) with God.
7. The (RAINBOW DUST COMET) is the sign of God's covenant with Noah.
8. The people of Babel wanted to build a (TOWER BOAT ELEVATOR).
9. God said to Abram, "Leave your homeland and your (BROTHER'S FRIEND'S FATHER'S) house.
10. Abram said to Lot, "We must not argue. We are (RICH FAMILY HAPPY).

# Journey To Canaan

You will need markers (paper clips, bottle caps or pieces of colored paper) and a coin. Put markers on HARAN. Flip the coin. If it lands head side up, GO. Move marker 1 space and say the correct word. Flip the coin again. You can keep going as long as you get the head side of the coin. When you get the tail side, STOP and give the coin to the other player. The first one to reach CANAAN is the winner!

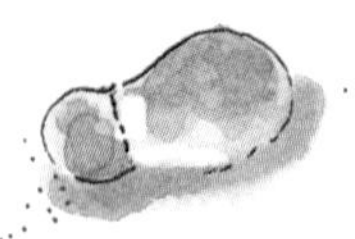
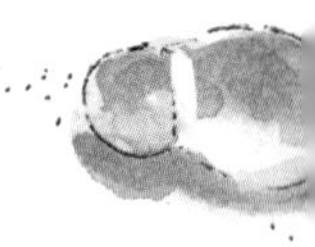

| **HARAN** | ADAM'S PARTNER | HE TRICKED EVE | IT WAS CREATED ON THE 4TH DAY |
|---|---|---|---|

THE 7TH DAY

HIS NAME MEANS "I GOT"

NOAH BUILT IT

## WHAT WOULD YOU DO?

**Settle the arguments to bring *shalom bayit*.**

"You wore my sweater and tore it!"

"You promised to be home by 5 o'clock"

"You're too little to play with me."

"You may not eat before dinner."

## CROSSWORD PUZZLE

What should we try to bring to our homes? To find out, fill in the words across. The answer is 1 down.

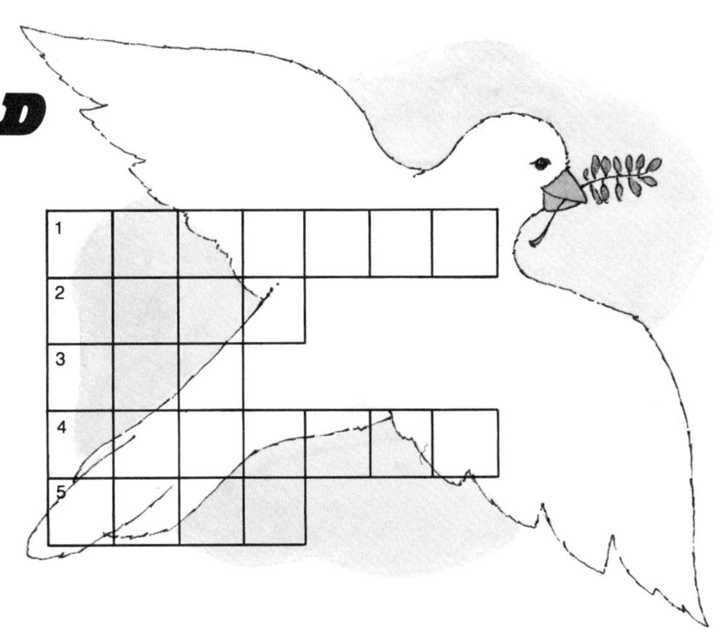


1. God made Eve to be Adam's__________.
2. God planted a garden in__________.
3. Noah built an__________.
4. God__________the world.
5. The snake was__________.

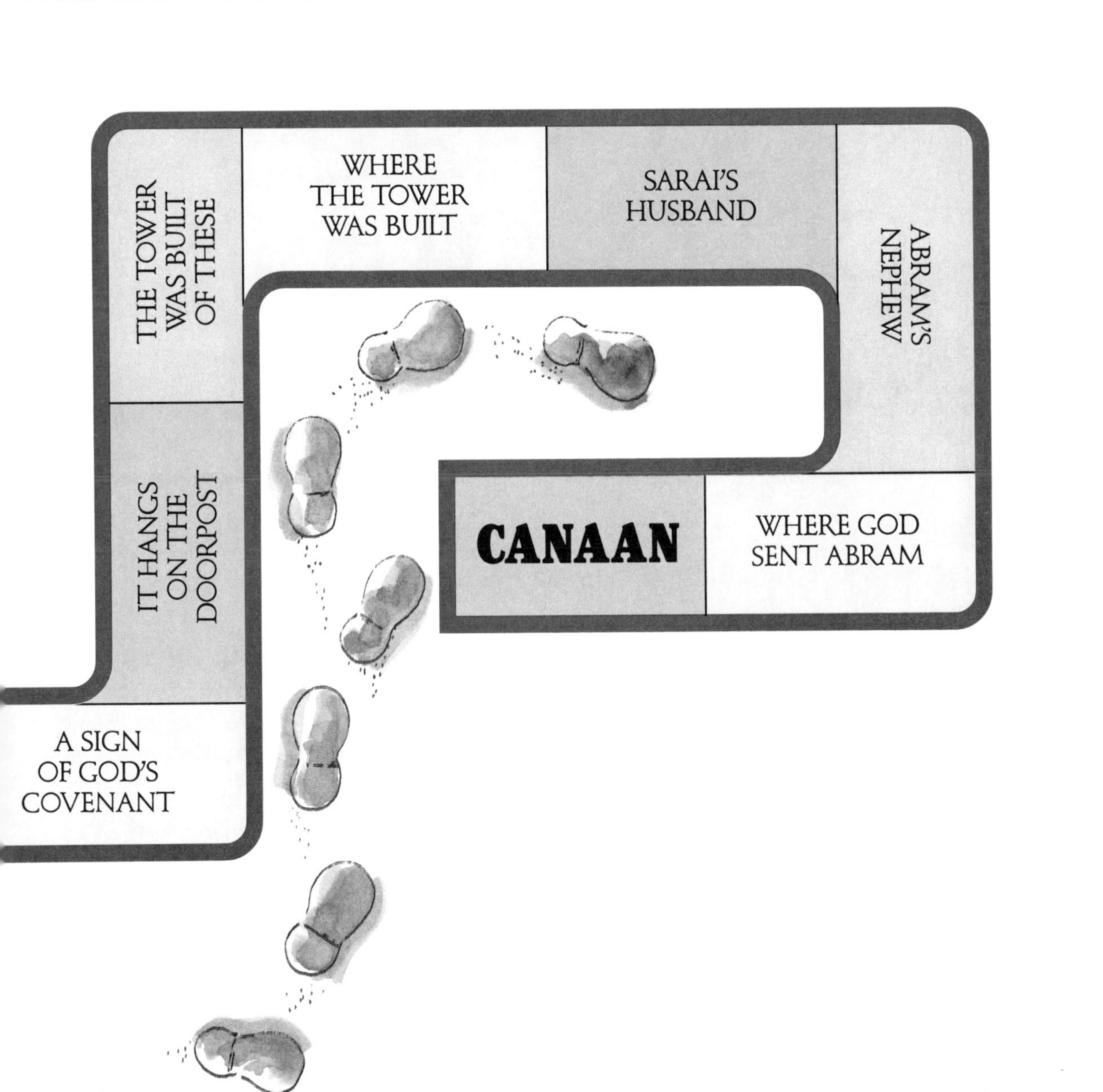

Genesis 18:1-19:29 בְּרֵאשִׁית

*Chapter 7*

# THE SAD TALE OF SODOM

Many years passed. Still Abram and Sarai had no children.

When Abram was ninety-nine years old, God said, "Walk in My ways and always do right. I will make My covenant between Me and you. Your new name shall be Abraham. Sarai's new name shall be Sarah. I will bless her. And I will give you and Sarah a son."

Abraham laughed long and hard. To himself, he thought, "Sarah and I are too old. Can we really have a son?"



God knew Abraham's mind. And God said, "Think what you like. You two shall have a son and you will name him Isaac, 'Child of Laughter.'" And God remembered Sarah. Sarah had a son, and Abraham called him Isaac. Sarah said, "God brought me laughter. Everyone who hears how I had a son in my old age will be happy with me."

It happened one hot afternoon. Abraham was sitting at the entrance of his tent when he looked up and saw three men nearby. He ran to welcome them. He bowed and said, "Please stay with me. Let me give you water and food."

Abraham and Sarah made a hot meal and placed it before their guests. When it was time for the guests to leave, Abraham walked down the road with them. They came to a cliff, and, looking down, they saw the city of Sodom. Two of the guests went down to Sodom, but one stayed behind with Abraham.

Now God thought, "Abraham is My friend. I shall not hide from Abraham what I am going to do."

Then God said, "Sodom and Gomorrah are very wicked cities. I can hear their evil even in the heavens. I will go down to see what they do. If they do evil, I will destroy them. But if they will learn to do good, I will forgive them."

Abraham stepped close to the edge of the cliff. He looked down at Sodom. He said to God, "You are the Judge of all the earth. You know it is not fair to destroy good people along with bad people. What if there are fifty good people in the city? Won't you forgive everyone if there are fifty good ones?"

God answered, "If I find fifty good people in Sodom, I will forgive the whole place. If I find fifty."

Abraham spoke up again. He said, "I am a very small thing, yet I dare to speak to God. What if there are forty-five good people? Will you destroy the cities because only five good people are missing?"

God answered, "If I find forty-five, I will not destroy the cities."

Then Abraham spoke once again: "What if you find only twenty?"

God answered, "I will not. If I find twenty."

Then Abraham said, "Do not be angry. I will speak one last time. What if you find ten good people there?"

And God answered, "I will not destroy the cities if I find ten good people."

That evening, two angels came to Sodom. Abraham's nephew, Lot, was sitting by the city gate. He welcomed them and said, "Please, spend the night at my house." He cooked dinner for them and they ate.

Just before bedtime, the people of the city gathered around Lot's house. Lot went out to talk to them. They shouted, "Bring us those two strangers. You know we always destroy strangers!"

Lot said, "I beg you, do not do such evil things."

But the people said, "Either we will destroy them or we will torture you!" They grabbed for Lot and started to break down his door.

Quickly, the angels pulled Lot into the house. They shined a light so bright that the townspeople were blinded. No one could even find Lot's door.

Early the next morning, the angels took Lot and his family outside. They cried, "Run for your life! Do not look back. If you do look back, you will die!" Then Lot and his wife and his daughters ran quickly toward the hills.

As the sun burned high in the sky, God rained fire out of heaven on the cities of Sodom and Gomorrah. The cities filled with flame. No one could escape. Just then, Lot's wife stopped and turned to look behind her. And she was turned into a rock of salt.

The next morning, Abraham hurried to the edge of the cliff. All he could see was a black cloud rising from the land like the smoke from an oven. The cities of Sodom and Gomorrah were gone. But God had listened to Abraham. God had rescued Lot.

WHAT DOES IT MEAN?

## Abraham...saw three men nearby.

Who were the three men that visited Abraham?

Our teachers say: They were really angels. One came to destroy the wicked cities of Sodom and Gomorrah. Another came to save Lot and his family. And the third was a messenger to Abraham and Sarah. Abraham called this one "God" because this angel spoke the word of God.

At first, Abraham did not know they were angels. But Abraham treated all strangers as guests. He welcomed them, just as Lot welcomed them in Sodom. It is not always safe to talk to strangers, but the story teaches another very important lesson. Being cruel to strangers is never the right thing to do.

WHAT DOES IT TEACH?

## Saving the Good People

God and Abraham made a bargain. God agreed not to destroy Sodom and Gomorrah if there were only ten good people in Sodom (the larger city). Even though there were not ten good people there, God rescued the only good people–Lot and his family.

As Abraham said, God is "the Judge of all the earth." God knows the heart of good people and takes special care of them. In the Torah, God even speaks about good people in a loving way. That is why God said, "Abraham is My friend." Look again at the story. What did Abraham do to be God's friend?

**The Plain of Mamre today: Nearby, Abram pitched his tent, greeted the three strangers, and argued with God.**

A LESSON ABOUT THE TORAH

# Why Was Lot's Wife Turned Into Salt?

Our bodies need salt, especially when we live in hot, dry places. When it is hot, we sweat a lot. Sweat is water and salt, so our bodies lose salt by perspiring. We must replace the salt we lose. In hot places like Sodom and Gomorrah, salt was very precious.

Our teachers say: Lot's wife was turned into a rock of salt because she was stingy like the other people of Sodom.

At dinner, Lot said to his wife, "Welcome our guests. Give them salt for their food."

But Lot's wife said, "I will not give them salt! I will not welcome them at all!"

Though she was unkind to them, the angels tried to save her. But she loved Sodom and its ways. Even while she was running away, she began to miss her evil friends. She refused to believe the angels. She thought, "Everything is fine in Sodom. I really want to go back." She turned around and suddenly she was turned into a rock of salt!

[Source: Rashi, Commentary]

**The Dead Sea: Along its banks stood the cities of Sodom and Gomorrah. The Bible calls it the "Sea of Salt." It is so full of salt and other minerals that nothing can live in it.**

**On the cliffs above the modern city of Sodom stands a lone column that people call "Lot's Wife."**

# MYSTERY WORD

Cross out any letter that appears two times.
Write the mystery word on the blanks to finish the sentence.

Sodom was a very wicked

______ ______ ______ ______

## ABRAHAM ARGUES WITH GOD

Abraham did not want God to destroy Sodom. God listened carefully to Abraham. Did you? Here are some of the words Abraham used. Try to put them in the correct order.

**FAIR IT PEOPLE NOT IS GOOD DESTROY ALONG TO WITH PEOPLE BAD**

Abraham said,

"________________________________________

________________________________________

________________________________________?"

# LOOKING FOR UNDERSTANDING

Underline the correct answer.

1. God told Abraham to name his son Isaac
   a. because Abraham and Sarah laughed when God said they would have a son.
   b. because God laughed when Abraham argued about Sodom.
   c. because people love to laugh.
2. God decided to destroy Sodom and Gomorrah because
   a. the people in the cities were doing too much good.
   b. the cities were too rich.
   c. the people in the cities were only doing evil things.
3. Abraham asked God to save the cities
   a. because Abraham liked looking down at them from the cliff.
   b. because the cities were good places to visit.
   c. because there might be good people in the cities.
4. God saved Lot and his family because
   a. the angels had more to say to them.
   b. they were kind to the strangers.
   c. they were part of Abraham's family.
5. Lot's wife was turned into a rock of salt because
   a. Lot looked back.
   b. she did not do what the angels told her to do.
   c. she never did anything right.

# MULTIPLE CHOICE

Circle the word that best completes the sentence.

1. God changed Abram's name to______________.

   **Isaac Abraham Sarah**

2. Abraham welcomed the three strangers and gave them______________.

   **clothes money food**

3. God decided to destroy the cities of Sodom and Gomorrah because they were______________.

   **empty evil noisy**

4. When the two angels came to Sodom, Lot was sitting by the______________.

   **well cliff city gate**

5. The townspeople told Lot to bring the strangers to them so that they could______________them.

   **destroy meet feed**

6. Lot's wife looked back and was turned into______________.

   **a loaf of bread a rock of salt a beehive**

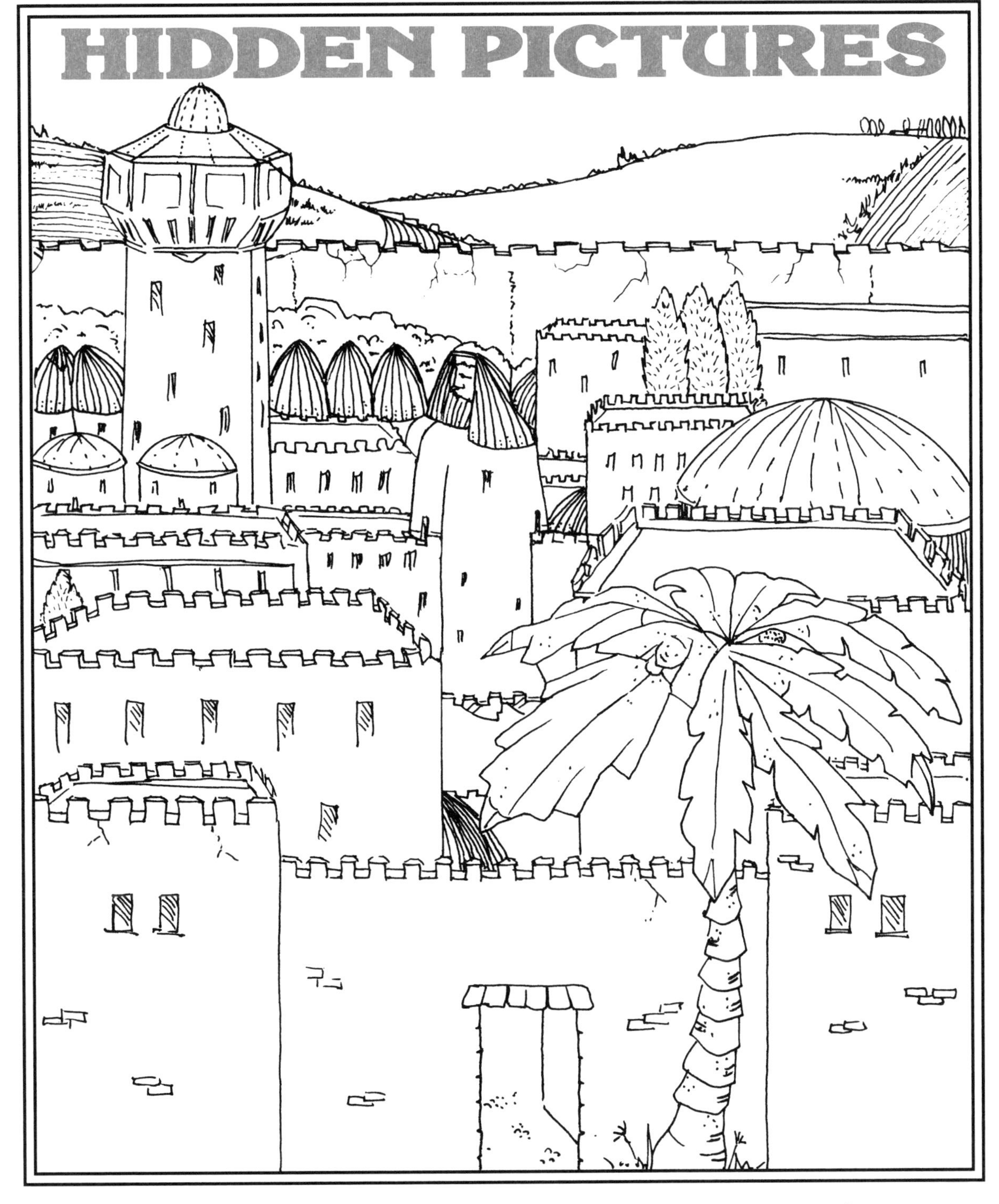




God agreed not to destroy the cities of Sodom and Gomorrah if ten good people were living in Sodom. There are two good people hidden in the city above. Can you find them? When you do, color them in. Then color the rest of the picture.

Genesis 22:1-17 בְּרֵאשִׁית

*Chapter 8*

# ABRAHAM'S GIFT TO GOD

God tested Abraham.

God said, "Abraham." And Abraham answered, "I am here."

God said, "Take your son–your favorite son Isaac that you love. Go to the land of Moriah, to a mountain that I will show you. Bring Isaac to the top of the mountain to burn him as a sacrifice."

Early the next morning, Abraham put a saddle on his donkey. He cut firewood for burning the sacrifice. Then he and two servants, and his son Isaac, started out. They walked in silence. Abraham's eyes stared straight ahead.

Three days passed. On the third day, Abraham looked up and saw the mountain. Abraham told the servants, "Stay here with the donkey. The boy and I are going up. We will worship and we will return."



Abraham took a flint stone to make the spark to light the fire, and he took a knife. He loaded the wood on Isaac. Together, Abraham and Isaac walked up the mountain.

As they climbed, Isaac said, "Father." And Abraham answered, "I am here, my son."

Isaac said, "We have the stone to spark the fire. And we have the wood. But where is the sheep to burn as a sacrifice to God?"

Abraham said, "God will take care of the sheep for the sacrifice, my son." And they walked on together until they reached the top of the mountain.

Abraham heaped up stones to make an altar. He put the wood on the altar. Then he tied Isaac with rope, and put Isaac on the altar on top of the wood. When everything was ready for the sacrifice, Abraham picked up the knife.

Suddenly, Abraham heard a voice. An angel of God called to Abraham from heaven. "Abraham. Abraham." And Abraham answered, "I am here."

The angel said, "Do not hurt the boy. For now I know that you love God. You have passed the terrible test. You would even give God your son, your favorite son!"

Abraham looked up. Out of the corner of his eye, he saw a ram. The animal was caught by its horns in a thick bush. Abraham took the ram and burned it as a sacrifice, in place of Isaac. And Abraham called that place Adonai-yireh, meaning "God sees." As they say,

From God's height,
There is true sight.

The angel spoke again. "I will tell you truly what God says. 'Because you have done this, I will place My blessing on you. I will give you many children—as many as the stars in heaven and the sands on the beach. Your children will be stronger than their enemies. And all the nations will bless themselves by your children because you listened to My voice.'"

WHAT DOES IT MEAN?

## Abraham took the ram and burned it as a sacrifice, in place of Isaac.

In ancient times, people believed that gods wanted sacrifices. The more important a god or idol was, the larger the sacrifice it wanted. People even thought some gods wanted a child as a sacrifice. These people really did sacrifice their children.

But the Torah teaches us that the One God loves human life more than sacrifices. Even in times of old, Jews never sacrificed human beings to God. They remembered the story of Abraham and Isaac.

WHAT DOES IT TEACH?

## What God Wants

The Torah says that God wants us to pass a test. We must show we are ready to serve God, just as Abraham did. We can pass the test if we obey God's commandments.

On the High Holy Days we blow the *shofar,* a trumpet made from the horn of a ram. Our teachers say that the sound of the *shofar* calls us to remember the commandments. It also reminds us of the test of Abraham and Isaac, when the ram was sacrificed in Isaac's place. Even though we hear this sound only on the High Holy Days, it is a sound that we can carry in our hearts all year round.

**The shofar is made of a ram's horn.**

**For Jews, the sound of the shofar is a symbol. When you hear it, what do you remember?**

The Sixth-century artist who made this mosaic used thousands of tiny colored tiles to tell the story of Abraham and Isaac. Look closely. What parts of the story can you find?

A LESSON ABOUT THE TORAH

## Can God Say One Thing and Mean Another?

Our teachers say: Abraham was confused. First, God said, "Burn your son as a sacrifice." Then God said, "Do not hurt the boy." Abraham said to God, "Do You say things and then change Your mind?"

God said, "I did not change My words at all. I did not say 'Burn your son as a sacrifice.' I said 'Bring him up to burn him as a sacrifice.' I only wanted to test you. All I told you to do was to bring Isaac up. You thought that I wanted you to burn him as a sacrifice. But I never wanted that."

[Source: Yalkut Me'Am Lo'Ez]

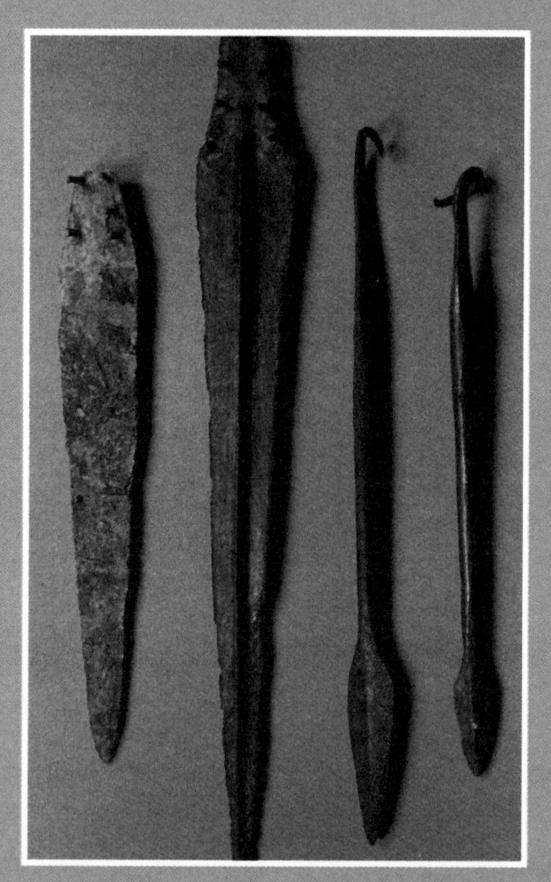

**In Bible times, these ancient sword blades were attached to handles made of wood or bone. Knives and swords were used as weapons and as tools.**

# MOUNTAIN MAZE

Help Abraham and Isaac reach the top of the mountain.

# A JIGSAW PUZZLE

Read the words on each puzzle piece. Write each word on a line to complete the sentence.

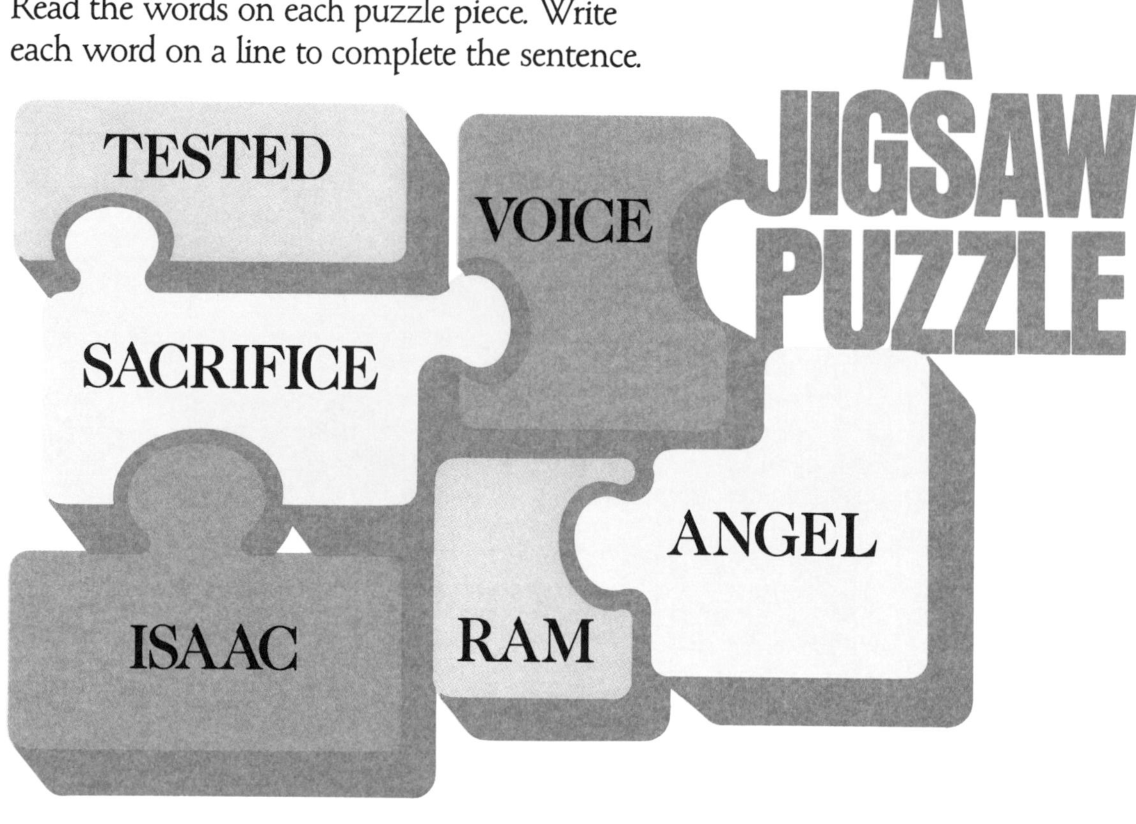


1. God ________________ Abraham.
2. ________________ was the son of Abraham and Sarah.
3. Abraham thought that God wanted him to ________________ Isaac.
4. Abraham burned a ________________ as a sacrifice.
5. God blessed Abraham because he listened to God's ________________.
6. An ____________ of God called to Abraham from Heaven.

## A WORD PUZZLE

Here are seven words from the story. One letter in each word is missing. Write the missing letter. Then read down to see who passed God's test.

IS☐AC
☐LESSING
SAC☐IFICE
☐LTAR
C☐ILDREN
W☐LKED
RA☐

# TRUE OR FALSE

Put an T in each box next to a true statement.

Put an F in each box next to an untrue statement.

| T | F | |
|---|---|---|
| | | 1. God tested Abraham. |
| | | 2. God told Abraham to take a sheep to the mountain. |
| | | 3. Abraham listened to God's voice. |
| | | 4. Abraham sacrificed a horse instead of Isaac. |
| | | 5. Abraham called the place Eden. |
| | | 6. God blessed Abraham because he listened to God's voice. |
| | | 7. Abraham learned that God does not want us to hurt one another. |

Challenge: Can you change the untrue statements to make them true?

# DOT TO DOT

Connect the dots to see what Abraham sacrificed.

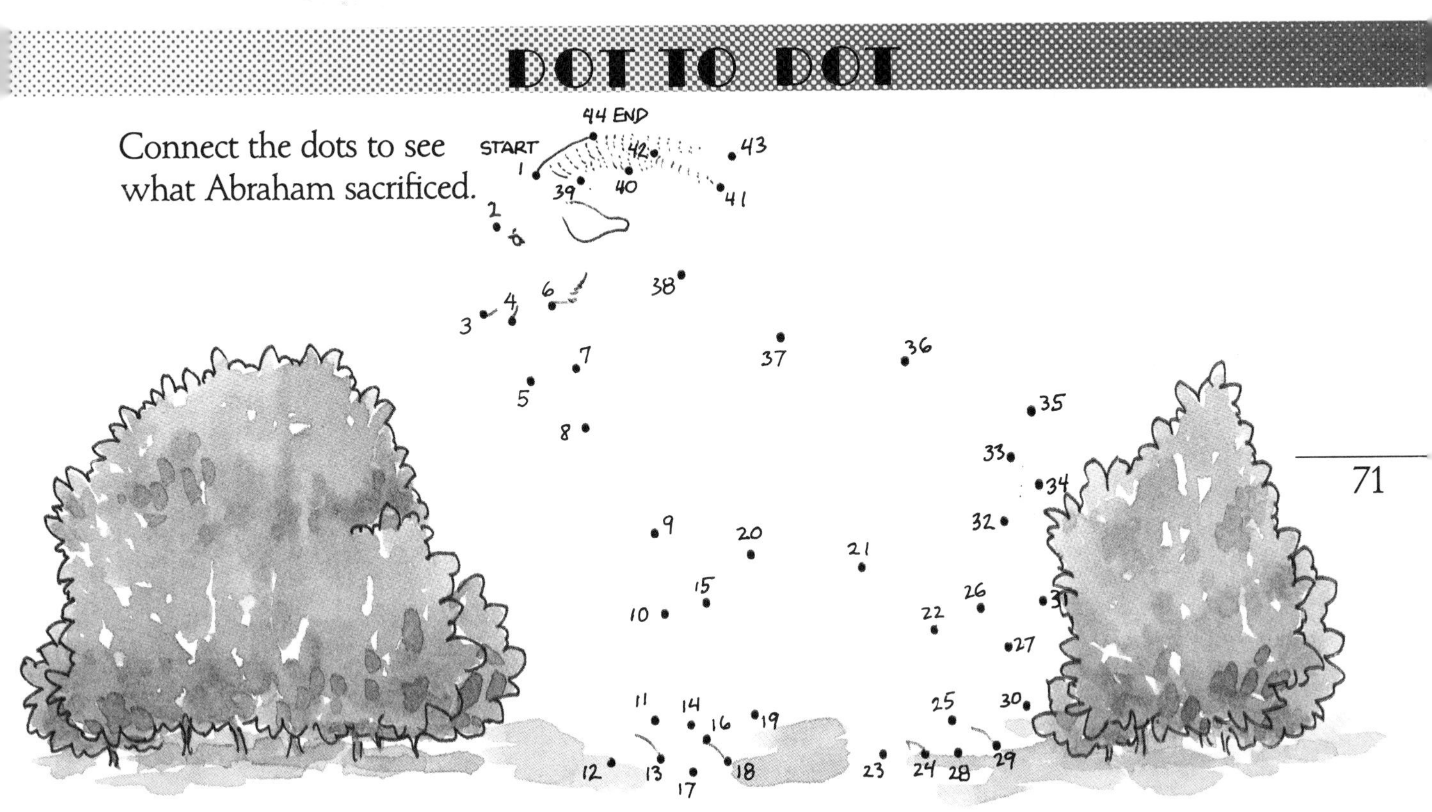

*Chapter 9*

# REBECCA

od promised the land to Abraham and his people, the Hebrews. Abraham and Sarah lived in many places in Canaan, from north to south, and back again. Abraham grew rich in the land, but he never owned any of it.

Sarah lived one hundred and twenty-seven years. Then Sarah died and Abraham cried mournful tears.

For the first time, Abraham needed to buy a piece of land. Abraham said to the Hittite people, "Sell me a cave where I can bury my dead." So Abraham bought the field and cave called Machpelah for four hundred shekels. Forever after, Machpelah belonged to Abraham as a place to bury. And that is where he buried Sarah.

God blessed Abraham in all things, but now Abraham was old. He called his servant and said, "Promise me that you will go to my homeland to find a wife for my son Isaac. But do not take Isaac there because God has chosen this land for my children." And the servant promised.

The servant took ten camels and many gifts. He took perfume, jewelry, and fine-looking robes. For many days he travelled to Abraham's country. At last, he stopped beside a well near the city of Nahor. It was evening, the time when the women of the city drew water from the well.

The servant said, "God of Abraham, bring me luck today. When a girl comes to get water, I will say, 'Please, let me drink from your jar.' Let one of the girls answer, 'Drink, and I will give water to your camels, too.' Then I will know she is the one You have chosen to be Isaac's wife."

Just then, along came Rebecca, Abraham's niece. She was as lovely as a morning sunrise. She lowered her jar to the water, and filled it. Abraham's servant went to her and said, "Please, let me sip a little water from your jar."

She said, "Drink." And when he finished drinking, she said, "I will also bring water for your camels."

The servant wondered, could his errand really be so easy? Rebecca made many trips to the well to bring water to the camels. When she was finished, the servant gave her gifts – a gold ring for her nose and bracelets of gold for her arms. He asked, "Is there room in your father's house for us?"

She said, "There is room for you to spend the night and plenty of feed for your camels." Then the servant spoke a prayer of thanks to God.

The girl ran ahead and soon her brother Laban came to the well. He said to the servant, "Come home with me. Everything is ready." So the servant went. The family brought food for him, but he said, "I will not eat until I tell my story." And he told all that had happened.

Then Laban and his father called Rebecca and asked, "Will you go with this man to be a wife for your cousin Isaac?" And she said, "I will." And her family blessed her.

Late one evening Isaac went out to walk and think. Then he looked up and saw the camels coming. He knew that the servant was bringing his new wife to him. And when Rebecca looked up, she saw Isaac.

She got down from her camel and said to the servant, "Who is that man coming to meet us?"

The servant said, "That is Isaac, my master."



Then the servant told Isaac everything he had done. And Isaac brought Rebecca to the tent that once belonged to his mother Sarah. He took Rebecca for his wife and loved her.

And that is how Isaac came to feel better, even though his mother had died.

**Doing chores can be hard, if we are forced to do them. Or they can be easy, when we choose to do them.**

WHAT DOES IT MEAN?

## And that is how Isaac came to feel better...

When someone we care about dies, we have to learn to live without that person. Abraham loved Sarah very much. When she died, he cried. But he went on to do some very important things. First, he bought a field and a cave in which to bury Sarah. This would become the family tomb–a place where he would be buried, too.

Then he thought about Isaac. Without his mother, Isaac would be very lonely. And Abraham knew what God taught Adam–it is not good for people to be alone. So Abraham sent his servant to find a wife for Isaac. When Isaac met Rebecca he, too, knew that she would be a good friend and wife for him. He would never again have his mother Sarah, but with Rebecca he would never again be lonely.

WHAT DOES IT TEACH?

## Doing What We Want to Do

Think of some of the tasks that you have to do–cleaning up after you play with your toys, straightening up your room and putting things in their place, even taking out the garbage. Most of the time, these seem like hard things to do. But sometimes even these chores can seem easy.

Rebecca's hardest chore was bringing water from the well. Like the chores that you have to do, she probably did not like this task. But our teachers say that when Rebecca decided that she wanted to bring water for the camels, the task suddenly seemed easy for her.

Doing chores is like that for all of us. If we only do them when someone forces us to, they seem hard. But when we choose to do them on our own, they suddenly seem very easy–and even fun to do.

**The walled-in building at the center of this photograph of Hebron is said to be the place of Abraham's "Cave of Machpelah."**

**Drawing water from the well was a woman's chore in the days of the Bible. At the well, the women of the town met and talked about the news of the day.**

A LESSON ABOUT THE TORAH

## A Test for a Wife

Abraham's servant asked God to help him find the right wife for Isaac. He prayed for luck. But he did more than pray.

Our teachers say: The servant made up a test to find exactly the right wife for Isaac.

He picked the prettiest girl. But that was not enough. He wanted to know what she was like on the inside. So he asked for a drink.

She could have said, "You are standing by the water. Help yourself!" Or she could have said, "Why pick on me? Ask one of the other girls for water."

Also, he asked for water from her jar. She could have said, "If I give it to you from my jar, I will have to go back down and fill my jar again. Let me get you a cup of water instead."

Last, he wanted the girl to say, "I will also water your camels." Watering the camels was a lot of work. Many girls would say, "If you have had enough water to drink, I will be on my way."

But Rebecca passed the whole test. She would make a good wife for Isaac. She was kind to people and kind to animals.

Finding the right wife for Isaac was more than "luck." It was work–the work of a very smart servant.

[Source: Malbim, Commentary]

**Jewelry, like these ancient pieces, was among the many gifts that Abraham's servant brought to Rebecca.**

# FILL THE BOXES

Put the first letter of each word in the box below its picture.

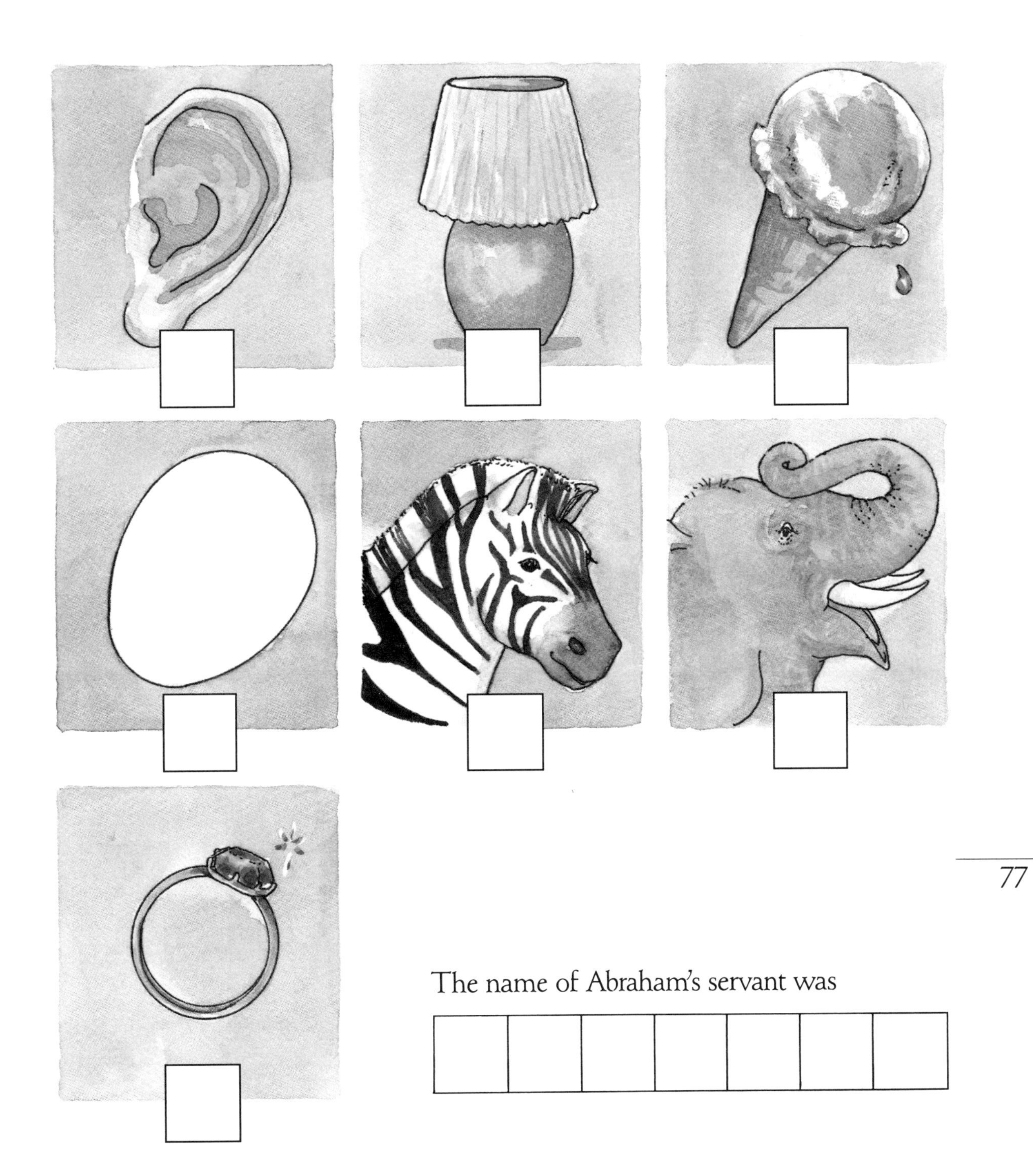

The name of Abraham's servant was

# Name Scramble

Put the letters in the correct order to see the names.

Abraham's son: __________ Isaac's wife: __________ Abraham's wife: __________ Rebecca's brother: __________

# REBUS

The serv- said, "God of Abraham, b- me luck 2-day. When a comes 2 get will say, 'Please, let me drink from your .' Let 1 of the answer, 'Drink & will give to your 2.' T- will know she is the 1 U have chos-N 2 -saac's wife."

# LOOKING FOR UNDERSTANDING

Underline the correct answer.

1. Abraham bought a piece of land (to farm) (as a cemetery) (to build a house on it).

2. Abraham asked his servant (to find a wife for Isaac) (to bring him some food) (to collect wood for a fire).

3. The servant knew that God chose Rebecca to be Isaac's wife because (God told him) (Rebecca was part of Abraham's family) (Rebecca passed the test).

4. Isaac felt better, even though his mother had died, because (his father said, "Feel better") (the servant told him to feel better) (he could share his love with Rebecca, his new wife).

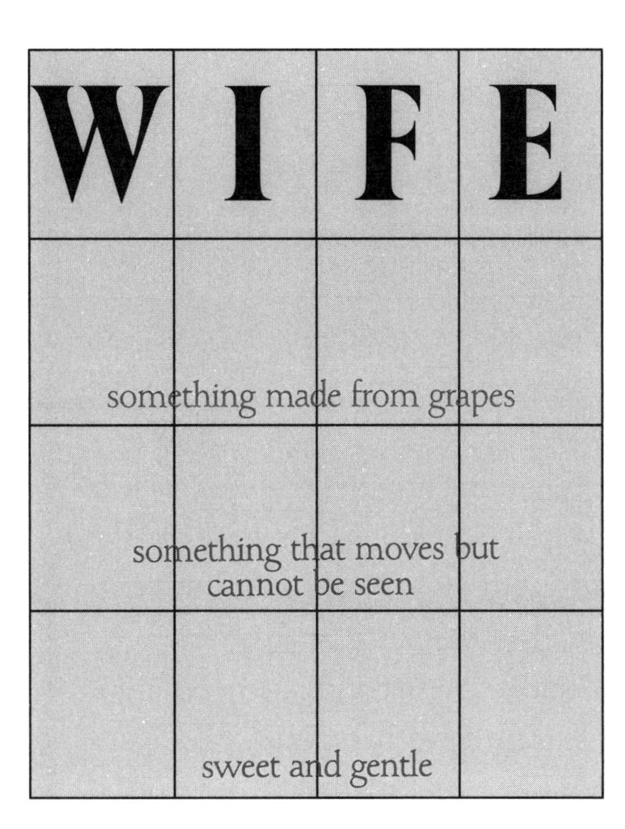


# CHANGE A LETTER

Abraham's servant found a good wife for Isaac. Can you do the same? You can change only one letter in each word, each time. There are clues along the way.

Rebecca was ______________ and caring. She was the right wife for Isaac.

Genesis 25:19-34;27:1-41 בְּרֵאשִׁית

*Chapter 10*

# TWINS AND TRICKS

Rebecca could tell by her pains that she had more than one child in her. She asked God why she suffered such pain.

God said, "Two nations are fighting inside you. One will be stronger. But the young one shall be the master." And when her time came to give birth, Rebecca had twin boys.



The first baby was red and covered with hair. Rebecca and Isaac called him Esau, which means "full of hair." The second baby came out holding Esau's heel in his fist. They called him Jacob, meaning "heel."

Esau loved the outdoors. He grew to be a mighty hunter. Isaac liked to eat meat from the hunt, so Esau became his favorite son. Jacob liked to help out at home. He was his mother's favorite.

Once Jacob was cooking stew when Esau returned from a hunting trip. Esau said, "I am so hungry! Let me wolf down some of that red, red stew!"

Jacob said, "First you must buy it from me. Sell me your birthright."

It was not a small thing to ask. A birthright was the larger share of things a father gave to his oldest son. But Esau said, "I am dying of hunger. What good is my birthright to me now? You can have it."

So Jacob served Esau a meal of lentil stew and bread. Esau ate and drank until he was full. And that is how Esau sold his birthright to Jacob.

Time passed and Isaac grew old. He could no longer see clearly. One day he called Esau to his bedside and said, "I may soon die. Go and hunt for me. Cook the meat the way I like it. Then I will give you the special blessing of the first-born son."



Rebecca was nearby and heard all that Isaac said. As soon as Esau left, Rebecca called to Jacob. "Listen carefully, my son," she said. "Bring a goat and I will cook it the way your father likes. You will take it to your father and he will give Esau's blessing to you."

Jacob was troubled. "Esau's skin is hairy," he said. "As soon as

Father touches my smooth skin, he will know it is a trick. Then he will curse me, not bless me."

But Rebecca had a plan. Jacob brought her a goat and skinned it so that she could cook the meat. Then Rebecca put Esau's best robe on Jacob. She covered Jacob's hands and neck with pieces of hairy goat skin. Then she gave Jacob the food to take to his father.

Jacob said to Isaac, "I am Esau, your oldest son. Sit up and eat the meat. Then give me my blessing."

Isaac said, "Come close. Let me touch and kiss you, my son." Jacob came close and Isaac took his hands.

Isaac was confused by the hairy skin. "The voice is the voice of Jacob," he thought. "Yet the hands are the hands of Esau." Isaac knew he could not trust his eyes, so he trusted his nose. He said, "Ah, but your robe smells like the robe of a hunter." Then Isaac gave Esau's blessing to Jacob.

A few minutes later, Esau came home from hunting. He, too, cooked a meal and brought it to his father. He said, "Father, sit up and eat. Then give me my special blessing."

Isaac said, "Who are you?"

He said, "I am Esau your oldest son."

Isaac's body rocked back and forth. "Who came before you bringing meat?" he shouted. "And I ate it! And I gave your blessing to him! Your brother tricked me!"

Esau said, "Jacob has grabbed my heel two times! First, he stole my birthright. Now he has stolen my blessing." So Esau hated Jacob. And Esau thought, "After my father dies, I will kill Jacob."

WHAT DOES IT MEAN?

## Isaac...could no longer see clearly...

The Bible does not say that Isaac was blind. It says he could not see clearly. That could mean many things.

Our teachers say: Perhaps Isaac could not see which of his twin sons would be a better leader for the Jewish people. But Rebecca could see that Jacob would be the best leader in the future. So she helped Jacob to trick Isaac and to steal the blessing from his brother.

WHAT DOES IT TEACH?

## Something for Today, Something for Tomorrow

Both the birthright and the blessing were important for the future of the Jewish people. But first Esau sold his birthright to Jacob for a pot of stew. Then Isaac gave his blessing to Jacob for a meal. Both times, the food seemed more important than the promise of things to come. In the same way, we sometimes forget the things we need for the future. It is easy to imagine that the things we need today are the really important things.

Using your money to buy candy may seem like the right thing to do this very moment. But maybe you should think twice before you do that. If you save your money, you might soon have enough for more important things. What things do you think are more important?

**Our teachers said that studying when young is like writing on clean paper—the writing is bright and clear. Studying when old is like writing on paper that has been erased many times—the writing is not as clear or as bright.**

A

What happened to the bowl that Jacob used to serve Esau his red, red stew? Clay pottery is a tough material, and even broken pieces do not easily crumble. Perhaps Jacob's bowl is among the many thousands that have been found by modern archaelogists.

In picture A, an archaeologist carefully brushes stone and earth away from pottery pieces. In picture B, the pieces are washed and labeled. If enough pieces are found, the pot may be put together like a puzzle (picture C). Then archaeologists make a drawing of the pot's shape to learn more about it and more about the place it was found (picture D).

A LESSON ABOUT THE TORAH

## The Larger Share, the Birthright

In Isaac's time, fathers gave twice as much of their land and possessions to the older child than they did to their younger children. This was called the "birthright." In the story, Jacob made Esau sell his birthright. Was Jacob just being greedy?

Our teachers say: Jacob had a good reason for wanting Esau's birthright. The child who had the birthright was also the one who became leader of the family's prayers.

Jacob knew that Esau did not love God, and would not pray. Esau did not believe in the covenant between God and Abraham. Esau would never be a good leader for the Jewish people. But Jacob did love God and did love prayer.

This was the real reason that Jacob wanted Esau's share. Jacob wanted to serve God as Abraham and Isaac had done before him. To do that, he needed the larger share, the birthright.

[Source: Rashi, Commentary]

B

C

D

# TODAY OR TOMORROW?

Look at the pictures below. What do you need today? What things will you need in the future?

# Do You Know Why?

Use the story to finish the sentences below.

Rebecca had great pain when she was pregnant because

______________________________.

Rebecca and Isaac called their first baby Esau because

______________________________.

They called the second twin Jacob because

______________________________.

Jacob wanted Esau's birthright because

______________________________.

Esau sold his birthright to Jacob because

______________________________.

Isaac gave Esau's blessing to Jacob because

______________________________.

Esau hated Jacob because

______________________________.

## WHAT DO NAMES MEAN?

In the Torah, many names of places and things have special meaning. Connect each of these names with its meaning.

| | |
|---|---|
| **ESAU** | **Heel** |
| **JACOB** | **Child of laughter** |
| **ADONAI-YIREH** | **I got** |
| **ISAAC** | **God sees** |
| **CAIN** | **Full of hair** |

Put a T in each box next to a true statement.
Put an F in each box next to an untrue statement.

## TRUE OR FALSE

- [ ] Rebecca suffered pain because she ate too much dinner.
- [ ] Esau sold his birthright for a meal.
- [ ] Isaac liked Esau better than his brother.
- [ ] Jacob was a mighty hunter.
- [ ] Rebecca covered Jacob's hands with hairy goat skin.
- [ ] Isaac gave the special blessing of the first-born child to Esau.
- [ ] Rebecca and Jacob tricked Isaac.

## DOT · TO · DOT

Connect the dots to see what Esau is doing.

START

27 END

# Think about it.

Can you draw a picture or write a sentence about something that is so important to you that you would never sell it?

Genesis 28:1-22;29:1-30;31:3 בְּרֵאשִׁית

*Chapter 11*

# JACOB TAKES TWO WIVES

saac sent for Jacob. Isaac said, "Your brother Esau hates you. He may try to hurt you. So, rise up. Go to the homeland of your mother and her brother Laban. Choose one of Laban's daughters to be your wife." And Jacob loaded the camels and went.

As the sun was setting, Jacob stopped for the night. He put a stone under his head as a pillow. As he slept, Jacob had a dream.

In his dream, he saw a stairway standing on the earth with its top in the sky. God's angels were going up and down the stairway. Suddenly, it seemed like Jacob was at the top of the stairs.

God stood beside him and said, "I am the God of Abraham and Isaac. I give this land to you and your children forever. Your children will be as many as the dust of the earth. They will spread out west and east, north and south. "Remember: I will watch over you wherever you go. And I will bring you back to this land."

Early the next morning, Jacob took the stone from under his head. He set it up as a place-marker and poured oil on it to make it holy. He called the place Beth-El, the House of God.

Jacob travelled on to Haran, to the place where his mother was born. He stopped at a well and spoke to some shepherds. "Do you know Laban the son of Nahor?"

They said, "Yes. And look, here comes his daughter Rachel with her flock."

Jacob drew water from the well and gave it to Rachel's sheep. Then he told Rachel that he was her cousin. Rachel ran home to tell her father Laban the news. Laban rushed out to welcome his nephew. He hugged Jacob, kissed him, and took him home.

Now Laban had two daughters. The oldest was Leah; and the youngest was Rachel. Jacob loved Rachel.

After one month, Laban said to Jacob, "You are my nephew. You can watch over my animals and take care of them. But how shall I pay you for working for me?"

Jacob said, "I will work seven years. At the end you will give me Rachel to be my wife."

Laban agreed. "That is good," he said.

Jacob worked seven years. He loved Rachel so much that the years seemed like days. Then Jacob said to Laban, "I worked for you as I promised. Now give me my wife."

Laban made a big feast. He invited everyone. In the darkness of the night he brought his daughter to Jacob. But in the morning light, Jacob saw that it was Leah and not Rachel!

Jacob said to Laban, "What have you done? I worked for Rachel! Why did you trick me?"

Laban said, "This is our way. The older daughter must be married first. Promise to work another seven years and I will give you Rachel, too."

So Jacob married two wives–Rachel and Leah. And Jacob worked seven more years for Laban.

WHAT DOES IT MEAN?

## And, look, here comes his daughter Rachel...

Hearing how Jacob found Rachel reminds us of how Abraham's servant found Rebecca. Just as Jacob's mother Rebecca came to the well, so too Rachel came to the well. Just as Rebecca was part of Abraham's family, so too Rachel was Jacob's cousin, a part of Abraham's family. Rebecca showed her kindness by giving water to the servant's camels and Jacob showed his kindness by giving water to Rachel's animals.

But there are many differences in the two stories. Laban was sly, and full of tricks. Though Jacob lived with Laban fourteen years, the two men never became good friends.

In the end, Jacob listened to God. He took Rachel and Leah, his two wives, and returned to the land where he was born.

**Because the Hebrews lived close to their herds and flocks, they respected people who were kind to animals.**

**When Jabob set up an altar, he probably tried to choose a stone with a large flat top. Later, altars were carved out of stone in a shape like the one in this picture. They were flat on top with handles or "horns" on all four corners.**

Since ancient times, brides have worn veils over their faces on their wedding days. Perhaps a veil like this tricked Jacob and made him think he was marrying Rachel.

WHAT DOES IT TEACH?

## What Has Five Wings and Is Made of Heaven?

Before Jacob left his homeland, he had a dream. He dreamed he saw a stairway with angels going up and down.

Are there really such things as angels? We can not know. But our teachers love to tell stories about them.

Our teachers say that every time God speaks, an angel is born. In Hebrew, the word for angel means "messenger." They say that angels are made of heaven. They say that angels are half-fire and half-water, with five wings. They say that God creates new angels every day, just to hear the angels sing the prayers. And they say that every angel has a special chore.

Two angels are with you all the time. One tells God the good things you do. The other is the angel of evil. This angel tells God the bad things you do. After a while, if you do many bad things, both your angels are evil. But if you do much good, both your angels are good.

Our teachers also say: God loves people who do good even more than God loves angels.

[Sources: Hag. 14a; p.R.H. 58a; Gen. R. 78:1; Ex. R. 21:4; Hag. 16a; Sanh. 59b]

A LESSON ABOUT THE TORAH

## Trick for Trick

Jacob knew that Laban was tricky. So Jacob took care to ask for Laban's younger daughter, Rachel, for his wife. Laban agreed. But Laban tricked Jacob anyway. How did this happen?

Our teachers say: When the time came for Laban to bring his daughter to Jacob's tent, Laban said to Jacob, "Put out the lamp. My daughter is very shy." And Jacob put out the lamp.

That night, whenever Jacob spoke to his wife, calling her "Rachel," Leah answered. But in the morning Jacob saw it was Leah.

Jacob said to Leah, "You tricked me. Last night I called you Rachel. And you answered!"

Leah said to Jacob, "You were my teacher. Isaac, your father, called you 'Esau.' And *you* answered! I learned how to trick you from you."

[Source: Gen. R. 70:19]

Help Jacob find the way to his mother's homeland.

# MISSING LETTERS

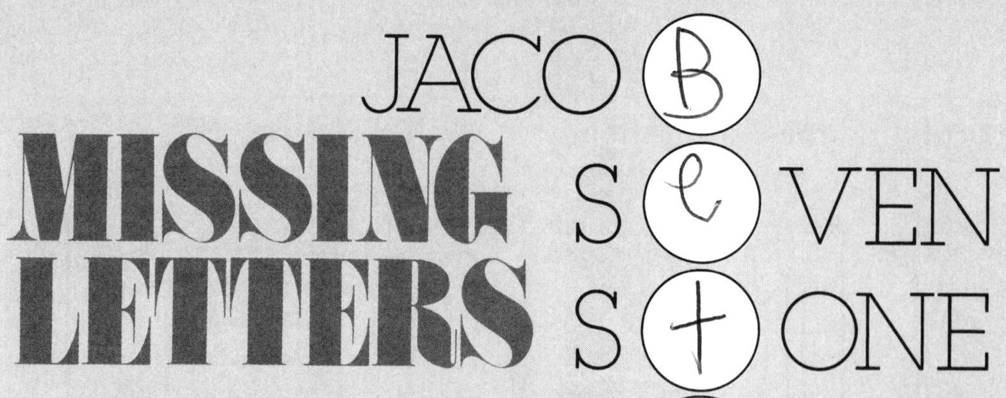

Here are six words that you know. Fill in the missing letters. Read down to see where Jacob placed a marker.

JACO (B)
S (e) VEN
S (t) ONE
RAC (h) EL
L (e) AH
(L) ABAN

Jacob called the place B e t h E L, the House of God.

# REBUS

As the  was setting, J- stopped. He used a  4 a  & slept. In his dream he  . Suddenly, J- was at the  of the . God said to him,  give this L-& 2 U & your children 4 -ever.

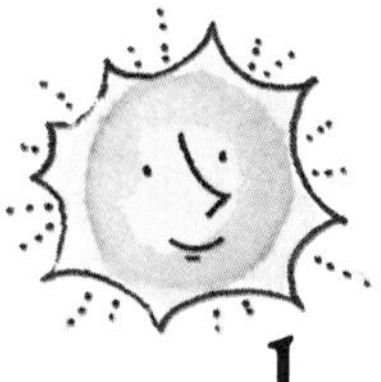

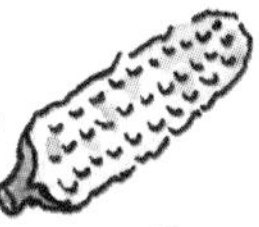

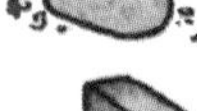

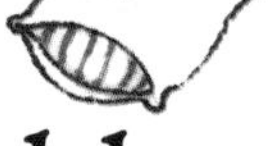

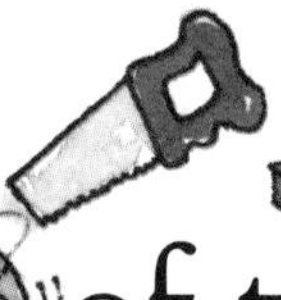

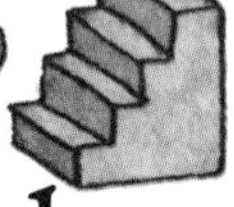

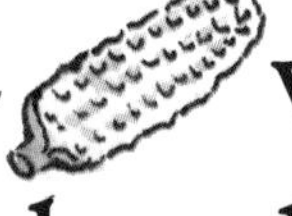

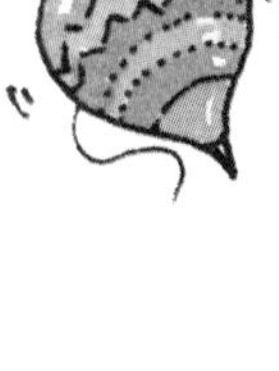

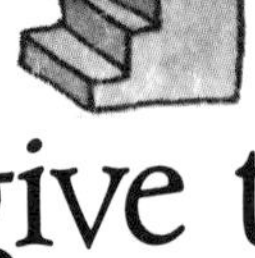

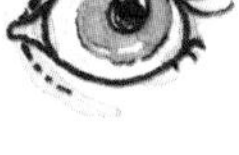

# QUESTIONS TO ANSWER

**Underline the best answer.**

1. Jacob went to his mother's homeland
   a. to work for Laban.
   b. to grow up and learn to stop tricking people.
   c. to choose a wife.
2. Jacob dreamed
   a. he saw a balloon fly up to heaven.
   b. he saw angels going down and up on a staircase.
   c. he was a rich man with a fancy house.
3. Jacob worked for seven years
   a. to build a tower to the sky.
   b. to earn enough money to go back home.
   c. to marry Rachel.
4. Laban tricked Jacob by
   a. sending him a camel dressed as a sheep.
   b. sending him Leah dressed as Rachel.
   c. sending him a telegram that said, "Hurry home."
5. Jacob tricked Isaac
   a. by hunting for food.
   b. by pretending to be Esau.
   c. by calling him Abraham.

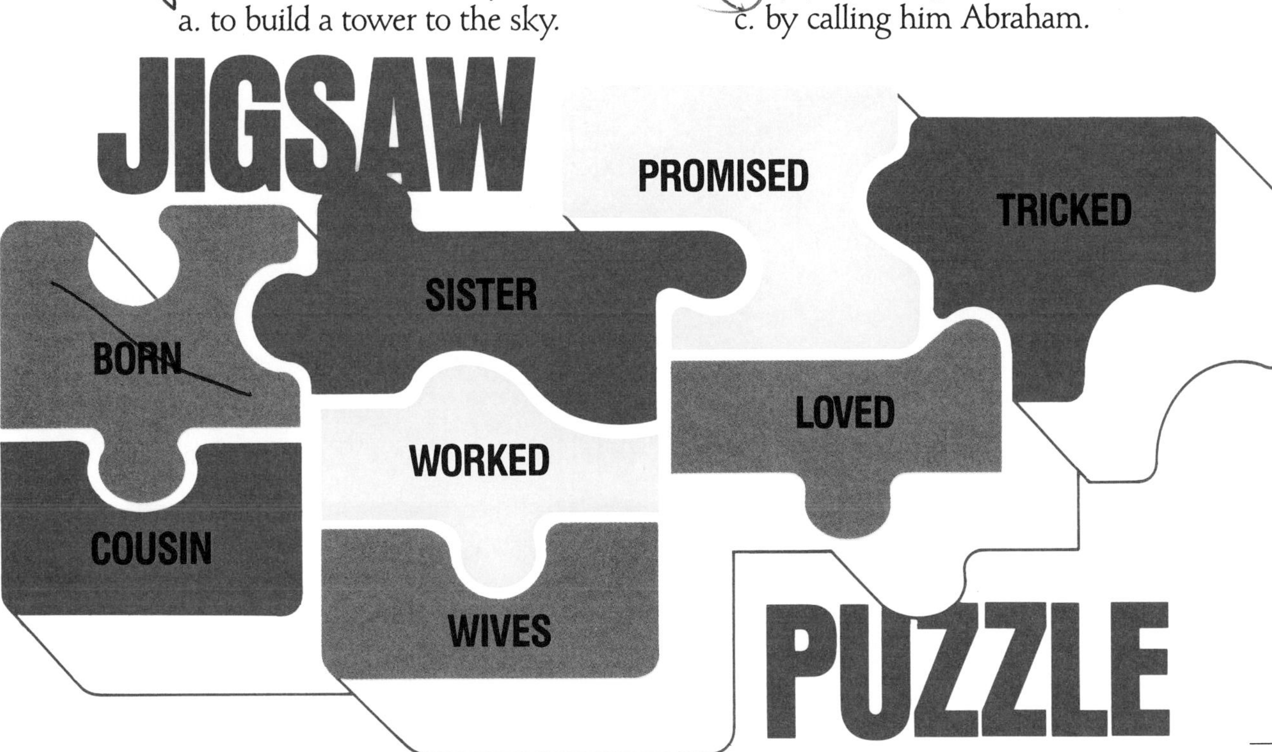




Jacob travelled to the place where his mother was __________. There he met Rachel, his __________. Jacob __________ Rachel. He __________ for seven years, but Laban gave him Leah, Rachel's __________, instead. Laban __________ Jacob. Jacob __________ to work for another seven years and Laban gave him Rachel, too. So Jacob married two __________ – Rachel and Leah.

*Chapter 12*

# JACOB RETURNS HOME

When Jacob's fourteen years of working were over, God said, "Return to the land where you were born. I will be with you."

Jacob took Rachel and Leah, his workers and his animals, and he set out for the Land of Canaan. He sent some workers ahead, saying, "Take a message to my brother Esau. Tell Esau that I stayed with Laban a long time. Now I have cattle, donkeys, sheep, and many workers. Ask Esau to be my friend."

In a while the workers returned. "We spoke to your brother Esau," they said. "He is coming to meet you. But four hundred men are coming with him. Perhaps Esau will kill you."

Jacob was very much afraid. He divided everything he had into two camps. He thought, "If Esau makes war on one camp, the people in the other camp can run away."

Then Jacob prayed. "God of my fathers, Abraham and Isaac. You said to me, 'Return home and I will be good to you.' Save me from my brother Esau. Otherwise he will kill all of us–even the mothers and children."



The next morning, Jacob sent gifts of goats and donkeys and camels and sheep to his brother Esau. He thought, "If I please Esau with gifts perhaps he will forgive me." That night Jacob took his family across the river. And Jacob spent the night alone.

But all was not quiet. Like a terrible dream, a stranger wrestled with Jacob all night. Sometimes it seemed that Jacob was winning; and sometimes it seemed that the stranger was. But when it grew clear that no one could win, the stranger gathered all his strength and twisted Jacob's hip. The pain was terrible, but still Jacob held on. At last, the stranger said, "You must let me go, for the sun is rising."

But Jacob said, "I will not let you go until you bless me."

The stranger said, "Here is my blessing: Your name will not be Jacob any more. You will be called Israel, 'the one who wrestles with God,' because you fought with God and with people. And now you know you can fight."

Jacob said, "Now tell me your name."

But the stranger said, "You must not ask me my name." And, as morning broke in the sky, the stranger left as mysteriously as he had come. And Jacob named that place Peniel.

By the light of the sun, Jacob saw Esau coming. Four hundred men were with him. Jacob acted like Esau was a mighty king. Seven times, Jacob bowed low to Esau as the two came closer together. Then, suddenly, Esau left his army and ran toward Jacob. Jacob was not afraid. He stood ready to fight for his life.

But Esau hugged Jacob and kissed him. And Esau said, "Why do you send me all these gifts? I have enough of my own. You can keep what is yours."

Jacob said, "No, please keep the gifts I sent you. You are kind to me. And seeing your face is like seeing the face of God."

And the twin brothers hugged again and cried tears of joy.

We can learn to love and help our brothers and sisters, instead of fighting with them.

WHAT DOES IT MEAN?

## You will be called Israel...

The Bible uses names to tell us about people and places. Abraham means "Father of Many Nations" and Sarah means "Princess." Isaac means "laughter" and reminds us of how Abraham and Sarah laughed at the news that they would soon be parents.

When big changes happened in the lives of these people, their names sometimes changed. Abram became Abraham, Sarai became Sarah, and in this story Jacob became Israel.

Of course, Jacob's new name became an important part of our lives. The Hebrews were soon called the "children of Israel," then the "Tribes of Israel," and later, *Am Yisrael,* the "people of Israel." And the Land of Canaan was known as *Eretz Yisrael,* "the land of Israel." And, in 1948, when our leaders had to choose a name for the new Jewish state, they proudly called it *Medinat Yisrael,* "the State of Israel."

The flag of the State of Israel flies among flags of modern nations, carrying the blessing of Jacob's new name into our time.

**This ancient carving shows two warriors making peace by hugging each other, just as Jacob and Esau did.**

A LESSON ABOUT THE TORAH

## Who Fought with Jacob?

Who was the stranger that fought with Jacob? Some teachers say the stranger was an angel. Every morning, the angels sing to God. And that is why the stranger had to leave early in the morning.

Some teachers say the stranger was really God. That is why Jacob called that place Peniel. Peniel means "the face of God."

Some teachers say Jacob was fighting Esau's angel. Like Esau, this angel was very angry at Jacob. The angel fought all night and could not win. So Esau's angel told Esau to make peace with Jacob And Esau did, the very next day.

Some teachers say the stranger was Jacob's own angel. The angel's name was "Israel." Jacob's angel fought all night to teach Jacob not to be afraid. Next day, Jacob did not have to fight against Esau. Jacob knew he was strong. He was strong enough to make peace.

Who was the stranger? We will never know. Our teachers told these stories to teach lessons. Who do you think the stranger was?

[Source: Gen. R. 77]

WHAT DOES IT TEACH?

## Love and Hate

Jacob sent a message to Esau, saying, "Ask Esau to be my friend." The Torah tells about real things. It tells the truth about brothers and sisters. It tells us how they sometimes fight and even hurt one another. At times, it even tells about how they hate one another the way Cain hated Abel and Esau hated Jacob.

In this story, the Torah teaches us a great lesson. Brothers and sisters who learn to hate can also learn to love. Part of growing up is learning how to change your mind. And part of growing up is learning to love your whole family, including brothers and sisters.

# CONNECTIONS

These pictures will remind you of people in the Torah.
Connect each picture to the name of the person.

REBECCA
ESAU
JACOB
ADAM
NOAH
LOT'S WIFE

# LOOKING FOR UNDERSTANDING

**Circle the best answer.**

1. Jacob returned to Canaan (to get away from tricky Laban) (to show his two wives to Esau) (to fight with an angel).
2. Jacob was afraid that Esau might (steal back the birthright) (give him the chicken pox) (kill him).
3. Jacob sent gifts to Esau to (wish Esau a happy birthday) (play another trick on Esau) (show Esau that they could be friends again).
4. Jacob's name was changed because (he wrestled with the angel) (he married two wives) (he did not want Esau to know him).
5. Jacob's new name is important because (it became a name for the Jewish people) (it is easy to spell) (it looks good in a book).
6. When Jacob and Esau met, (Jacob wrestled with Esau) (Esau asked Jacob about his new name) (Esau forgave Jacob and made peace with him).

Connect the people who go together.

| | |
|---|---|
| ABRAHAM | EVE |
| ADAM | REBECCA |
| ISAAC | LEAH |
| CAIN | SARAH |
| JACOB | ESAU |
| RACHEL | ABEL |

# REVIEW QUIZ

Circle the word that best completes the sentence.

1. God sent Adam and Eve out from____________.
   Babel    the Garden of Eden    Canaan
2. God punished Cain because he ____________his brother.
   loved    killed    hated
3. In Noah's time, God sent a ____________to destroy all living things on the earth.
   fire    raven    flood
4. In Babel, the people built ____________.
   an ark    a tower    a well
5. Rebecca was chosen to be Isaac's wife because she was____________.
   beautiful    wicked    kind
6. Jacob went to his mother's homeland to find a____________.
   camel    farm    wife
7. Jacob and Esau became____________.
   wrestlers    cousins    friends

## Numbers

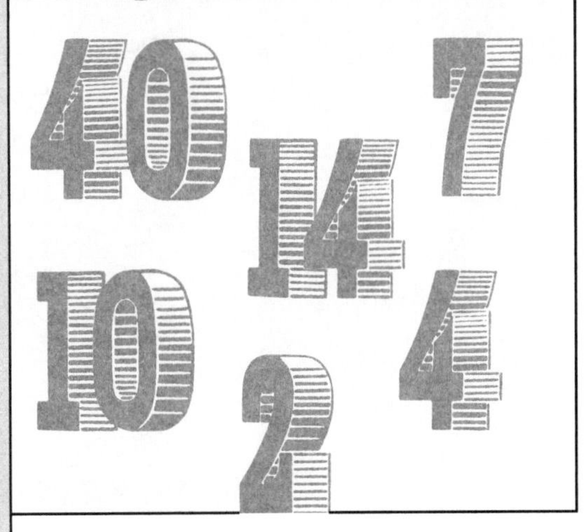


Can you complete each sentence with the correct number?

1. God created the world, then rested on day____.
2. In Noah's time, the flood waters rose for____days.
3. God sent the people of Babel to the____corners of the earth.
4. God would not destroy the cities of Sodom and Gomorrah if____ good people were found there.
5. Rebecca had____sons.
6. Jacob worked for Laban for____ years.

Genesis 35:22-29;37:2-35 בְּרֵאשִׁית

*Chapter 13*

# JOSEPH'S COAT

ow Jacob had two names. Sometimes he was called Jacob. And sometimes he was called Israel. Jacob had twelve sons: Reuben–his oldest, Simeon, Levi, Judah, Issachar, Zebulun, Joseph, Benjamin, Dan, Naphtali, Gad, and Asher. They were called the children of Israel.

Jacob's sons watched over their father's goats. Joseph was seventeen years old. He was Israel's favorite son. Israel took pieces of many fabrics and sewed them together to make a colorful coat for Joseph. This made Joseph's brothers very jealous.

One night, Joseph had a dream. He told his brothers about it. "In my dream," he said, "we were tying bundles of grain together. Suddenly your bundles made a circle and bowed down to mine."

This made his brothers angry. "Do you want us to bow down to you?" they asked. And they hated Joseph even more.

Joseph dreamed again. "In this dream," he told his father and brothers, "the sun, the moon, and eleven stars bowed down to me."

Now, Joseph's father grew angry. "What kind of dream is that?" Israel asked. "Do you want all of us, even your father and your mother to bow down to you?"



One day, Israel said to Joseph, "Your brothers are in the field watching the flocks. Go and find them. See what they are doing. See how the goats are. Then come back and tell me."

From far away, his brothers saw Joseph coming. "Here comes that dreamer," they said. "Let's kill him. We can say that a wild animal ate him."

Only Reuben tried to save Joseph's life. "No," he said. "Let's not kill him. Let's just throw him into that deep hole." As he left the camp, Reuben said to himself, "I will come back later tonight. I will take Joseph out of the pit and bring him safely home."

Just then Joseph came into the camp. His brothers grabbed him and pulled off his coat of many colors. Then they threw Joseph to the bottom of the pit.

Later, as the brothers were eating, they heard the tinkling of camel bells. A caravan of traders was passing nearby on its way down to Egypt. "Let's sell Joseph to them," Judah said. "Then we will not have to kill him. After all, he is our brother." And they all agreed.

Quickly, they pulled Joseph from the pit. They sold him to the traders for twenty pieces of silver. The caravan took Joseph to Egypt to sell as a slave.

When Reuben returned that night, he found the pit empty. "Oh, no," he thought, "I am too late. Joseph is dead." To his brothers, he said, "I am the oldest. Father will blame me. What can I do?"

So they took Joseph's coat and dipped it into goat's blood. Then they sent the coat to Israel with the message: "We found this. Is this Joseph's coat?"

Israel cried out. "This is my son's coat! A wild beast has eaten Joseph. My son is dead!"

Israel mourned for many years. His sons and daughters tried to help him forget Joseph, but he refused. He said, "I will mourn for my son to the day I die."

WHAT DOES IT MEAN?

# A Caravan of traders was passing...

A caravan was a long line of camels and people travelling together. Some of the camels had riders. Others were loaded with jugs of water for the trip and many things to sell.

In the days of the Torah, caravans crossed the Land of Israel from the far north down to Egypt and back. These caravans carried spices and silver to Egypt and brought back gold and cloth.

Often a caravan took slaves to sell to the Egyptians. The slaves were women and children or soldiers captured in a war. Or they were people who borrowed money and could not pay it back. At times, they were even people who chose to live as slaves.

**In the desert, camel caravans were more popular than donkey caravans because camels carry their own water supply.**

A strong, young boy like Joseph was worth a lot of money. The traders gave Joseph's brothers twenty pieces of silver. But they planned to sell Joseph in Egypt for a much higher price, for gold.

**Tel Dothan: Not far from here, the brothers threw Joseph into the pit. A tel, like the "hill" in this photograph, is really the ruins of many ancient cities built one on top of another.**

WHAT DOES IT TEACH?

## The Coat of Many Colors

The brothers hated Joseph because Joseph was sent to visit the camp and then tell Jacob if the brothers were doing a good job. They hated him more because he dreamed of ruling over them. But they hated him most of all because of his coat of many colors. Why should a little thing like a coat make them so angry that they wanted to kill Joseph?

For a long time, we did not know the answer. Then we discovered some paintings on the walls of tombs in Egypt. In the paintings, only the chiefs of the tribes wore coats with beads or coats of many colors. Joseph's coat was probably like the ones in the paintings. So now we know that when Jacob made Joseph this coat, he was really saying that Joseph was the chief of the brothers. That is what made the brothers so jealous that they were ready to kill.

**Cut wheat is tied in bundles and left in the field where the sun dries it. These were the kind of bundles that were in Joseph's dream.**

**A wall painting from Egypt shows Canaanite men and women wearing many-colored robes. Joseph's "coat of many colors" may have looked like one of these.**

A LESSON ABOUT THE TORAH

## Jacob and the Wolf

Our teachers told this story:

Jacob saw the coat covered with blood. He thought Joseph was killed by a wild beast. He was sad. But he was angry, too. Very angry.

He said to his sons, "Go. Search for the body of Joseph. If you find it, I will bury my son. If you do not find it, bring me the first wild animal you find. I will kill that animal, because a wild animal killed my son."

The brothers went hunting. They knew they could not find Joseph's body, for he was still alive. So they caught a wolf and brought it to Jacob.

Jacob took the wolf by the neck and said, "Why did you kill my son Joseph?"

Lo and behold! The wolf opened its mouth and words came out. "I am innocent," the wolf said. "I did not kill your son. I come from a land far away. I am looking for my lost cub. I do not know if the cub is alive or dead. But today, while I was looking, your sons grabbed me. Now my life is in your hands."

Jacob was ashamed. He said to the wolf, "It is good that God made you speak. You are not guilty. I forgot what Abraham taught: 'You shall not kill the good ones with the evil ones.' Now, go and look for your cub. And I will keep looking for Joseph. May God bless us both so we will both find our children."

[Source: Sefer HaYashar]

**Woven threads from a striped, many-colored cloth made nearly two thousand years ago. The dry desert air protected the cloth from that time to this.**

# JOSEPH'S BROTHERS

The names below belong to Joseph's brothers. The letters in each name are correct, but some letters have changed places. Can you write the names correctly?

REUNEB

1 ______________________

NOSEIM

2 ______________________

LVEI

3 ______________________

UJDAH

4 ______________________

ISACHRAS

5 ______________________

ZELUBUN

6 ______________________

DAG

7 ______________________

ASHRE

8 ______________________

DNA

9 ______________________

NAPTHAIL

10 ______________________

MBENAJIN

11 ______________________

## Looking for Understanding

1. What did Joseph dream?
2. Why were the brothers jealous of Joseph's coat?
3. Why did Jacob decide not to kill the wolf?
4. Are you ever jealous of your brothers or sisters or friends? What makes you jealous?

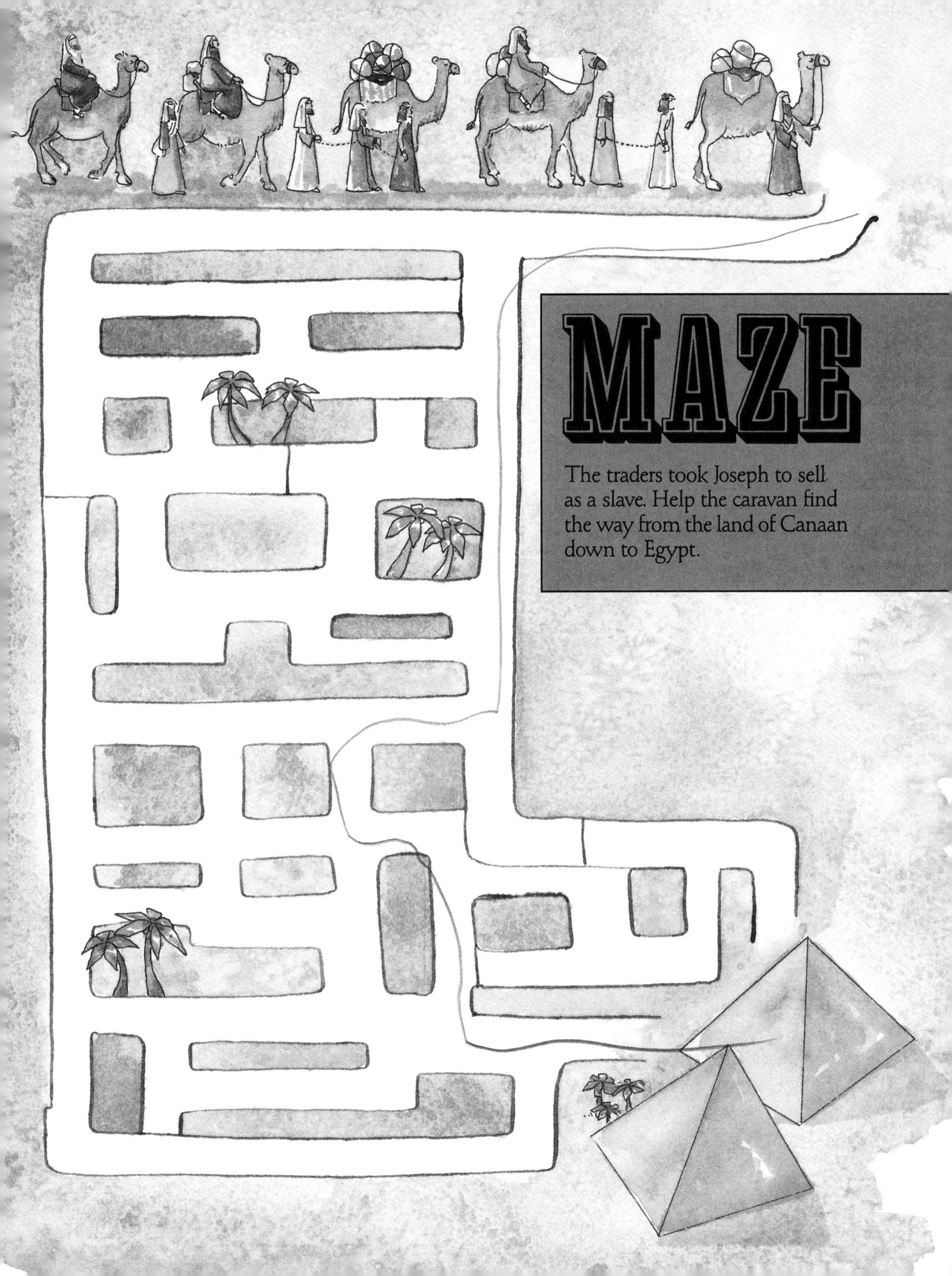

MAZE
The traders took Joseph to sell as a slave. Help the caravan find the way from the land of Canaan down to Egypt.

## WHAT IS TRUE

The story explains how Joseph's brothers came to hate him. Some of the reasons below are true. Mark the true sentences with a "T" and put an "F" before the false ones.

- [ ] Jacob gave Joseph special food like the food he made for Esau.
- [ ] Joseph carried tales to Jacob about how his brothers behaved.
- [ ] Joseph slept in a nicer tent than his brothers.
- [ ] Joseph had more pairs of sandals than his brothers.
- [ ] Joseph had more gold and silver than his brothers.
- [ ] Joseph was given a special coat.

## COMPLETE THE STORY

Use these words to fill in the blanks:

**KILL FAVORITE SOLD JEALOUS PIT COAT ANIMAL**

Joseph was Jacob's ______________ son. Jacob made a special ______________ for Joseph. This made the brothers very ______________. They decided to ______________ Joseph. But they changed their plan and threw him into a deep ______________ instead. Later, they ______________ Joseph to a caravan going down to Egypt. They told Jacob that Joseph had been eaten by a wild ______________.

# JOSEPH'S COAT

Jacob made a colorful coat for his son Joseph.
Can you design and color this coat as you think it might have looked?

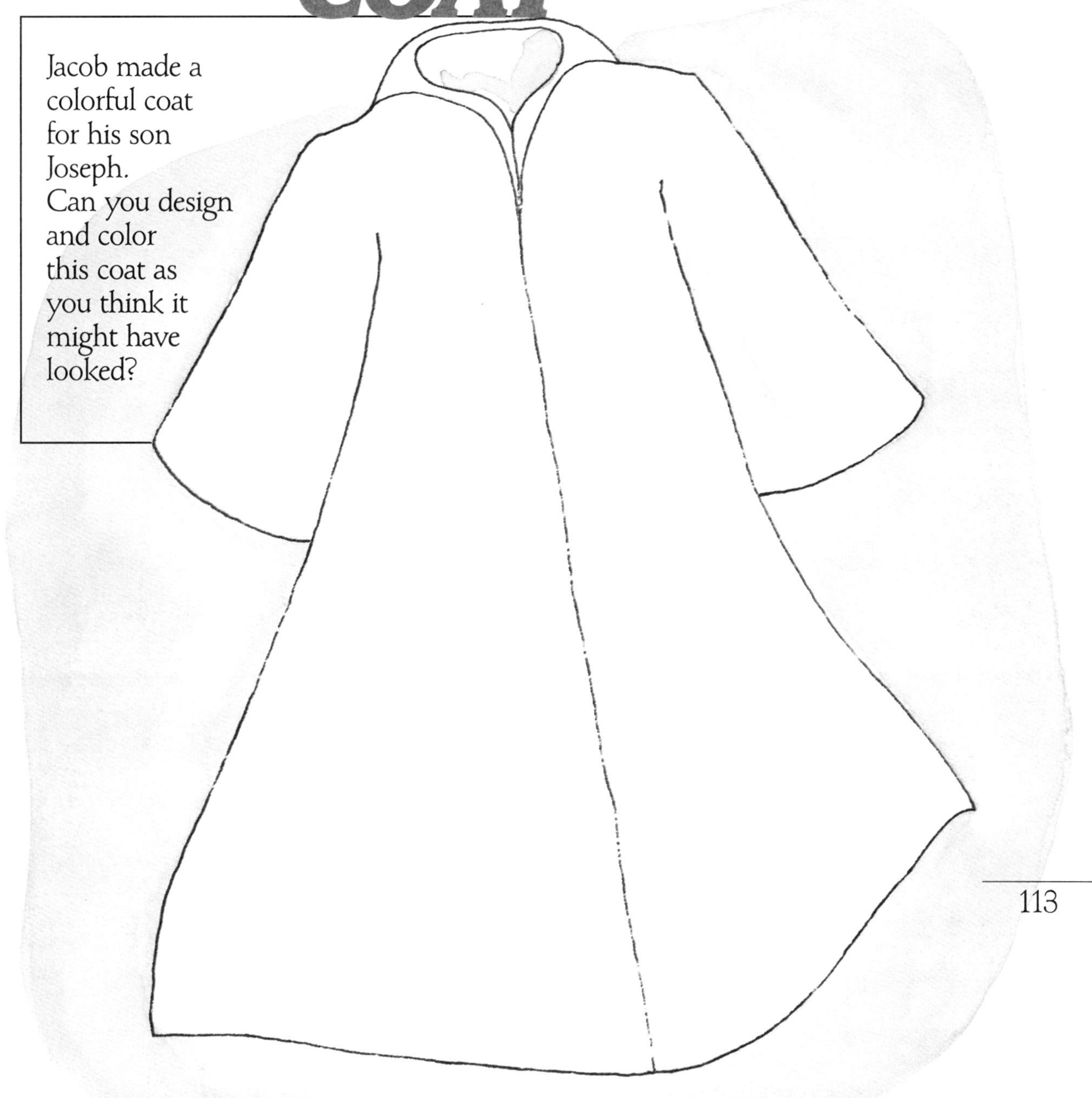

Genesis 39:1;39:19-41:57 בְּרֵאשִׁית

*Chapter 14*

# JOSEPH AND THE DREAMERS

gypt was ruled by a king called the Pharaoh. It was Pharaoh's chief butler who bought Joseph to be his slave.

Joseph worked hard to be a good servant. But one day the chief butler grew very angry with Joseph and threw Joseph into Pharaoh's jail.

Time passed. It happened that Pharaoh grew angry at his cupbearer–the man who poured his wine. Pharaoh put the cupbearer in jail with Joseph. The cupbearer had a dream and the dream told a story. He asked Joseph, "Can you tell me what my dream means?"

Joseph said, "God can tell! Let me hear it."

The cupbearer said, "In my dream there was a vine with three branches. All at once, the buds became blossoms and the blossoms became grapes. I made wine for Pharaoh's cup and gave the cup to Pharaoh."

Joseph said, "Your dream means this: In three days time, Pharaoh will take you from jail. Then you will be Pharaoh's cupbearer once again. Please, remember me. Ask Pharaoh to set me free for I have done nothing wrong."

It happened just as Joseph had said. Except that when the cupbearer was free, he forgot all about Joseph.

Two years went by. One night, Pharaoh dreamed a dream that woke him. He went back to sleep, but soon he had another dream like the first. The next morning Pharaoh called for all his magicians and all his wise men. But no one could tell Pharaoh the meaning of his dreams. It was then that the cupbearer remembered Joseph.

Quickly, Joseph was taken from the jail. The Pharaoh's barbers gave him a haircut and the Pharaoh's tailors gave him new clothes. Then Joseph was brought into the great palace.

Pharaoh said, "I hear you can tell a dream by listening to it."

Joseph answered, "Not I! But God will help Pharaoh."

Then Pharaoh said, "In my dream, I was standing by the Nile River when seven fat cows came out to eat the reeds. Then seven ugly, skinny cows followed. The skinny cows ate the fat ones. But after they ate, they were still as ugly and skinny as before! Then I awoke.

"I went back to sleep," Pharaoh continued. "I dreamed that I saw seven fat ears of corn on one plant. Close by, seven thin ears of corn grew. And the thin ears of corn swallowed up the fat ones."



Joseph explained, "Pharaoh's dreams are one and the same. The fat cows and fat ears of corn are seven years of plenty. The skinny cows and thin ears of corn are seven years of hunger. God has told Pharaoh what will happen. Egypt will have seven good years. Afterwards, will come seven years of terrible hunger. Dreaming a thing twice means God will do it soon."

Joseph went on, "Let Pharaoh choose someone wise to rule over Egypt's fields. The food of the good years must be saved for the years of hunger or else the people of Egypt will starve and die."

Joseph's plan pleased Pharaoh. Pharaoh said, "We will not find another better than Joseph, for God's spirit is in him."

So Pharaoh made Joseph a ruler of Egypt, and Joseph ruled all the land. For seven years, he saved the grain. The grain was plentiful like the sands on the shores of the sea. Then the seven years of hunger came.

When the people of Egypt cried out to Pharaoh for food, Pharaoh said, "Go to Joseph. Do what he says!" And Joseph gave out the food, a little at a time.

The terrible years of hunger were everywhere. All the world came to Joseph in Egypt to buy food.

## WHAT DOES IT MEAN?

# "God will help Pharaoh."

Pharaoh asked Joseph to explain his dreams. Joseph said, "Not I! But God will help Pharaoh." Our sages say: God sends dreams to teach us. Joseph knew that God had already helped Pharaoh by sending these two dreams. The dreams were sent to Pharaoh because only Pharaoh could use them to save the people of Egypt from hunger.

The Torah seems to say that dreams are personal. Your dreams teach you things you need to know. Even a bad dream can help you to grow stronger. As Joseph said, dreams are God's help.

## WHAT DOES IT TEACH?

# Good Listening

All of Pharaoh's magicians and all of his wise men could not explain his dreams. Our sages say: this is because they were not good listeners. They heard only what Pharaoh said in words. When Pharaoh said that he had two dreams, they believed him. They tried to tell him the meaning of two different dreams. So all the things they said made no sense to Pharaoh.

Joseph also heard Pharaoh say that there were two dreams. But he listened very carefully. And that is how he discovered that both were really one and the same dream. If you want to help people by listening to them, you must first listen to their words. But then you must also try to hear what their words mean. Joseph was a good listener.

**To "read" this Egyptian wall painting, begin on the right. Farmers used oxen to plow. They cut the wheat. They tossed it in the air to separate the grain. And they brought sacks of grain as offerings to the Pharaoh.**
**Even today, Arab farmers toss wheat so that the wind will separate it. The heavier grain falls to the ground, while the lighter stalks and husks are blown aside.**

A LESSON ABOUT THE TORAH

# How Joseph Came to Be in Jail

Joseph was very handsome. Our sages say: he even liked to look in a mirror and admire himself.

In the days when Joseph worked for Potiphar, Pharaoh's chief butler, the butler's wife used to look at Joseph and think how handsome he was. She wanted Joseph to admire her, too.

One day, when she was alone with Joseph, she tried to hug and kiss him. Joseph knew that this was wrong. He started to run away from her. But as he ran, she caught hold of his coat and pulled it off.

Now the butler's wife hated Joseph. When Potiphar came home, his wife said, "The slave named Joseph tried to hug and kiss me, but I would not let him."

Potiphar was surprised. He said, "I do not believe you. Joseph is a good man."

His wife showed him Joseph's robe. She said, "Here is the proof. The slave left this in my room!"

Seeing the robe, Potiphar grew very angry. "I will throw the man into prison," he said. And that is how Joseph came to be in jail.

[Source: Gen. R. 87:4]

**During the seven good years, Joseph collected the grain of Egypt and stored it in huge silos like the ones shown in this model.**

**Statue of an Egyptian official and his wife. Potiphar and his wife may have had a "family portrait" like this one.**

# FILL THE BOXES

Put the first letter of each word
in the box below it.

The king of Egypt was called the

_______________________________

# CHOOSE THE BEST

Circle the word that best completes the sentence.

1. Egypt was ruled by a king called ____________.
   Henry  Pharaoh  Peniel
2. The chief butler threw Joseph into Pharaoh's ____________.
   pool  kitchen  jail
3. Pharaoh's magicians and wise men did not know the meaning of his ____________.
   dreams  name  clothes
4. Joseph told Pharaoh that there would be seven years of ____________.
   bad luck  dreams  hunger
5. All the world came to Egypt to buy ____________.
   pyramids  idols  food

# WHAT'S IN YOUR DREAMS?

Some people dream by night and other people have day dreams. Have you had an interesting dream? Use the space above to draw it or write about it.

# WHO SAID IT?

Joseph was a good listener. Are you? Choose from this list of people to tell who said each of the sentences below.

**JOSEPH THE CUPBEARER**

**PHARAOH THE CHIEF BUTLER THE PEOPLE OF EGYPT**

1. "I will throw Joseph into jail," said____________________.
2. "There is a man in jail who will know what Pharaoh's dreams mean," said__________________.
3. "In my dream, I was standing by the Nile River," said __________________.
4. "God has told Pharaoh what will happen," said________________.
5. "We are hungry. Give us food," said____________________.

# Dot to Dot

Connect the dots to see what Pharaoh dreamed.

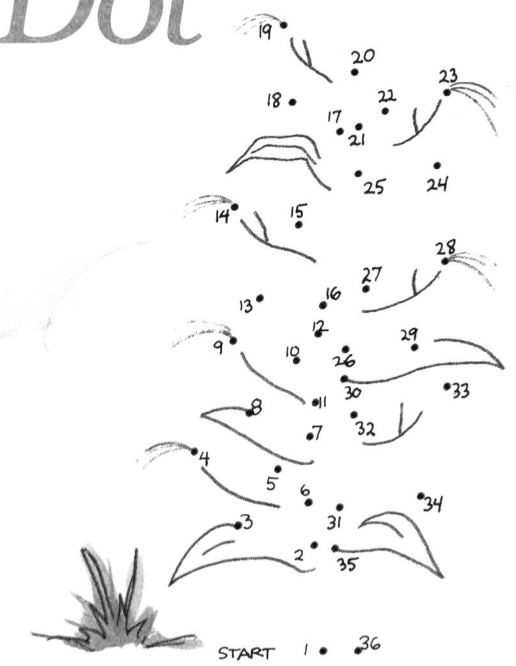


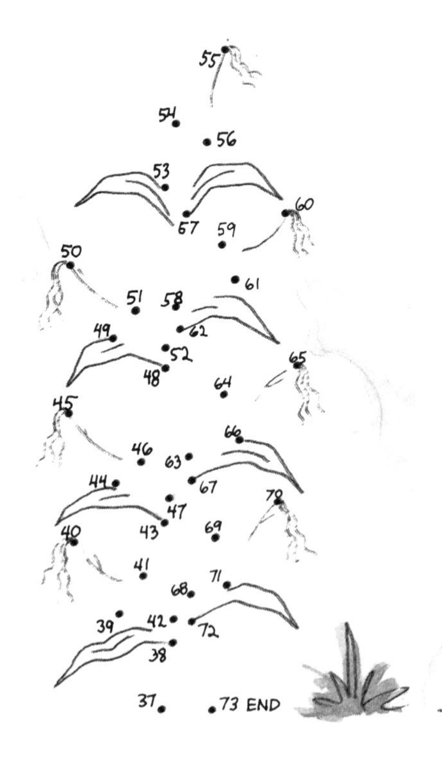

# Do you know why?

Only one sentence in each group is correct. Circle the one that is true.

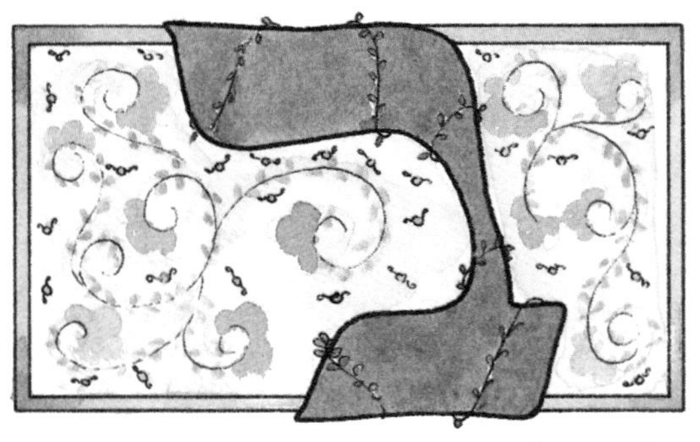

1. The cupbearer remembered Joseph because Joseph gave him a good haircut in jail.
2. The cupbearer remembered Joseph because Joseph told him the meaning of his dream.
3. The cupbearer forgot all about Joseph forever.

1. Joseph did not understand the meaning of Pharaoh's dreams, so he made up a story to tell the Pharaoh.
2. Joseph read about Pharaoh's dreams in the *Egyptian Daily News.*
3. Joseph told Pharaoh that God would help explain the dreams.

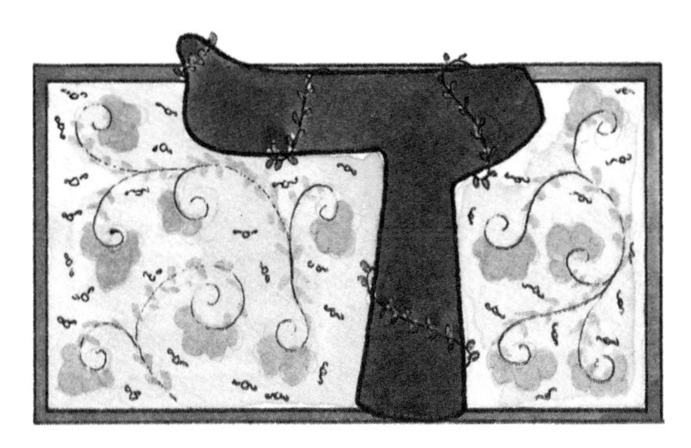

1. Pharaoh made Joseph the chief magician of Egypt.
2. Pharaoh told Joseph to send for Jacob.
3. Pharaoh made Joseph a ruler of Egypt.

1. All the world came to buy food in Egypt because food was cheap there.
2. All the world came to buy food in Egypt because there was no food anywhere else.
3. All the world came to buy food in Egypt because Egypt was holding a big food sale.

Genesis 42:1-43:34;45:4-28;47:27 בְּרֵאשִׁית

*Chapter 15*

# COME DOWN TO EGYPT

Hunger was everywhere in those terrible years, even in the land of Canaan. Now Jacob had many sons and daughters and they had many children of their own. There was not enough food. Jacob knew there was food in Egypt, so he sent ten of Joseph's brothers to buy food and bring it back. Only Benjamin, the youngest, stayed at home.



Thus the brothers came to Egypt, a rich land of giant statues and dazzling city gates. They were taken to a grand room filled with people all coming to buy food. Every wall was covered with paintings alive with color. At one end of the room, steps led upward to a throne. On the

throne sat the man called "the ruler of Egypt." They bowed to him, keeping their faces low to the ground.

The brothers did not know it was Joseph seated on the throne high above them. But Joseph recognized his brothers and remembered how he dreamed long ago that one day they would bow down before him. Yet he pretended not to know them.

Joseph said, "You look more like spies than shepherds!"

"No, my lord, " they said, "We come only to buy food. We are honest people, and all sons of one man."

Joseph said, "I will test you. I will fill your sacks with grain. Then, nine of you will go and bring me your youngest brother. The one called Simeon will stay here with me."

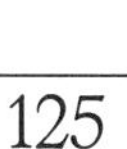



With heavy hearts, the nine brothers went home and told Jacob all that had happened.

Jacob said, "Joseph is gone. Simeon is gone. And now you want to take Benjamin. Why do these things always happen to me? You must not return to Egypt."

But as the weeks turned into months, the hunger in Jacob's camp grew worse. The food from Egypt was gone. Jacob said, "Go again and buy food. Take gifts for the ruler of Egypt. Take Benjamin, too."

Once again, the brothers went down to Egypt. Once again, they bowed before Joseph.

This time, Joseph said, "I command you: Come to lunch at my house." The brothers were troubled, but Joseph's servant said, "Do not be afraid." And he brought Simeon to them.

The brothers gave Joseph all the gifts Jacob had sent. Joseph looked closely at Benjamin, his youngest brother, and tears of joy filled his eyes. Joseph asked, "How is your father? Is he well?" They spoke of Jacob and the children of Israel.

Joseph told each one where to sit. He placed the oldest one at the table nearest to him and each one next by age. The brothers were puzzled. How did the ruler of Egypt know their ages?

Suddenly Joseph stood up. In his heavy robe, he looked like a mighty Egyptian statue. He said, "I am your brother Joseph. Do not be sad that you sold me into slavery. God sent me ahead to save many people from dying of hunger. God has made me like a father to Pharaoh. Now, hurry home. Tell my father all you have seen. Bring my father here with all speed."

Then the brothers gathered close around Joseph to see if it was truly he. They hugged and kissed and laughed and cried all at the same time.

As soon as they could make ready, they hurried back to Canaan. With joy in their hearts and excitement in their eyes, they told Jacob, "Joseph is still alive. Yes. *He* is the ruler of all Egypt!"

Jacob cried tears of happiness. "It is good! My son Joseph is still alive! I must see him before I die. Gather all my family together. Pack our tents on camels and bring the herds of sheep and goats in from their pasture. We must not delay!"



And that is how Israel come to live in the land of Egypt. The children of Israel bought land. They had children. And they grew to be many on the earth, just as God had promised.

WHAT DOES IT MEAN?

## "God sent me ahead..."

Many things, some good and some bad, happened to Joseph in Egypt. Yet he was not angry that his brothers had sold him into slavery. Joseph believed that this was a part of God's plan. If Joseph had not been in Egypt, many people would have died in the years of hunger.

We do not always know why bad things happen. Sometimes we just have to believe as Joseph did, that God has a plan, and that each one of us is a part of it. By doing the best we can, we may suddenly find that we have done something very important for us and for the world.

WHAT DOES IT TEACH?

## Forgiving Others

One of the hardest things to do is to forgive other people when they have hurt you. The story of Joseph and his brothers teaches us about forgiving. If Joseph had been another kind of person, he might have taken revenge on his brothers. He could have refused to sell them food. It would have been a cruel thing to do. But revenge is always cruel.

All the same, forgiving is always difficult. Our sages say: we must try hard to be like Joseph. After a fight is over, after an argument is ended, we have to do our best to forgive and forget.

**This ancient wall painting of Canaanites bringing gifts to the Pharaoh, helps us imagine how Joseph's brothers looked when they brought gifts to Joseph in Egypt.**

**Forgiving others makes everyone feel better.**

## A LESSON ABOUT THE TORAH

# The Deaths of Jacob and Joseph

**The modern artist Marc Chagall made stained-glass windows showing the symbols of the twelve tribes of Israel. Taken from his designs, these Israeli postage stamps remind us of the twelve tribes that became one nation.**

Before Jacob died, he gave his blessing to all twelve of his children. He also blessed the children of Joseph – Ephraim and Manasseh. To Joseph, he gave the treasured blessing. This was the blessing passed from Abraham to Isaac to Jacob. Joseph became the leader of the people, even though he was not the oldest child.

Jacob said to Joseph, "When I die, do not bury me in Egypt. Carry me up to the Land of Canaan. Let me sleep beside Abraham and Isaac, my fathers." Joseph promised. And when Jacob died, the twelve brothers travelled to Canaan and buried Jacob in the cave that Abraham bought in Machpelah.

Joseph lived a good life in Egypt. When he was about to die, he said to his family, "God will remember you. When God rescues you from Egypt, take my body with you."

Many years passed. The children of Israel became a nation, just as God promised Abraham. They filled the land of Egypt. When Moses led the people of Israel out of Egypt, they took Joseph's body with them. So all the family of Abraham was buried in the land of Israel.

# THE WALLS OF EGYPT

The best artists in Egypt were wall painters. Here is a sample of a painting from one of the walls. Can you draw an Egyptian wall design below it?

# TRUE OR FALSE

**Mark each true sentence with a "T" and put an "F" beside each false one.**

The brothers came to Egypt to sell food. ☐

Joseph remembered his brothers. ☐

The brothers bowed down to Joseph. ☐

Joseph would not give his brothers food. ☐

Reuben stayed in Egypt when the brothers went home. ☐

Jacob never let his sons return to Egypt because they did not need more food. ☐

When the brothers learned that the "Ruler of Egypt" was Joseph, they ran away. ☐

When Jacob found out that Joseph was still alive, he traveled to Egypt. ☐

# LETTER SCRAMBLE

Make the letters below into a word that tells what Joseph did.

O F G
R A V E

Joseph ____________ his brothers.

# OPPOSITES

Each word in the first column means the opposite of a word in the second column. Use lines to connect the opposites.

| | |
|---|---|
| **hunger** | **revenge** |
| **terrible** | **plenty** |
| **rich** | **sadness** |
| **punishment** | **poor** |
| **forgiveness** | **reward** |
| **joy** | **wonderful** |

# MISSING LETTERS

Joseph remembered his brothers. Can you? One letter is missing from each name. Fill in the missing letters to see what Jacob did before he died.

___ ENJAMIN

___ EVI

ASH ___ R

___ IMEON

IS ___ ACHAR

Z ___ BULUN

___ AN

Jacob ______________________ his children.

Exodus 1:1-2:10 שְׁמוֹת

*Chapter 16*

# MOSES IN THE BASKET

Years without number went by. A new Pharaoh ruled over Egypt. He did not remember Joseph and all the good Joseph had done.

Pharaoh said to his people, "Look, these people called Israel grow many and strong. Perhaps they will make war against us and kill us. Let us make them slaves."

So Pharaoh put the Israelites to work making bricks and building great cities. But the harder they worked, the stronger they became. And Pharaoh grew frightened.

At last, Pharaoh sent out an order, saying, "If the Hebrews give birth to a baby girl, she shall live. But if they give birth to a boy child, he shall be put in the river and drowned."

These were dark days for the people of Israel. Many children were killed. Mothers and fathers everywhere wept in sadness. Just then, among the Israelites, Amram and his wife Yochebed had a baby boy. Yochebed hid her son, keeping him safe for three months. But the time came when he grew too large to hide.



Yohebed had a plan. She took reeds from the river and wove a basket. Inside and out, she covered the basket with tar, making it into a little ark. She placed her baby son in the basket. Then she took the basket

down to the river and set it out to float. Yochebed said to her daughter Miriam, "Come back and tell me what happens." Miriam hid in the reeds by the riverside. She watched the basket and wondered what would happen to her baby brother.

That afternoon, the Pharaoh's daughter came to the river to bathe. Out of the corner of her eye, she saw the basket floating in the short reeds. When she opened the basket, a baby reached out its tiny hands to her. Pharaoh's daughter took the baby gently in her arms and held it close. "This is a Hebrew child," she said.

Miriam saw this and came out of hiding. "O, Princess," she said, "I know I can find a Hebrew woman to help you care for the child."

"Yes," said Pharaoh's daughter, "for I shall keep this child as my own."

Miriam went home and told her mother all that had happened. Miriam and Yohebed hurried to the palace gate. Pharaoh's daughter met them and said, "Take the child and feed and care for him. When he is older, bring him back to me and I will raise him up to be a prince of Egypt."

Yochebed did just as Pharaoh's daughter asked. When the time came, she brought the baby boy back to the palace and Pharaoh's daughter took him as her own son. And Pharaoh's daughter named him Moses, which means, "pulled from the water."

WHAT DOES IT MEAN?

# "I shall keep this child as my own..."

Pharaoh's daughter truly loved Moses. She gave him everything, just as if she were his real mother. So Moses grew up in the palace of Pharaoh as an Egyptian prince. He wore fine robes. He learned to read and write. He studied the stars until he knew the night sky. He studied the books of wisdom of the Egyptians. He studied the geography of the Land of Egypt. All these things would be important when Moses led the people of Israel out of Egypt. Like all the princes of Egypt, Moses was trained to be a leader.

Whatever you want to do in life, you have to train for it. If you want to be a dancer or a doctor, an artist or an astronaut, there are things you must learn. Like Moses, the best time to start learning these things is while you are still growing.

**What do you want to do? Whatever it is, you must train for it. The best time to train is now, while you are growing.**

**The Nile River is Egypt's lifeline. Egyptians farm along its shores, and sail it from one end of Egypt to the other. Among the thickly-growing reeds of the Nile, the Egyptian princess found baby Moses in his ark.**

Slaves make bricks in this ancient wall painting. To make them, water is mixed with dirt and straw to make clay. Next, the clay is molded in the shape of a brick and left to dry in the sun.

WHAT DOES IT TEACH?

## Children Are Important

Like Pharaoh's daughter, almost everyone loves babies. But there are some grown ups who do not like children. Often these are people who think that only the things that grown ups do are important. But they are wrong.

Children make all the difference in the world. Children decide what the world will be like tomorrow. Children dream of the wonderful things that can be done and they set out to do these things. They change the world as they grow.

Even while you are still a child, you can make a difference in the world. You can make your parents proud of you. You can make your family happy. You can make your home and school a better place by the way you behave. All you have to do is try to be the best that you can be.

A LESSON ABOUT THE TORAH

## Moses and the Sabbath

Our sages say that Moses was very wise, even while he was still a boy. Once he saw the children of Israel working as slaves. He saw that they were treated badly by the Egyptians. And he decided to do something about it. He went to see his adopted father, the Pharaoh.

Like a child with a question, Moses asked, "What is the best way to make sure that an animal works?"

The Pharaoh answered, "Give the animal food and water and exercise and rest."

Moses said, "Your answer is good, mighty Pharaoh. But look at the slaves building your cities. They are given food and water and exercise. But they are given no rest. Surely, they would work better if they could rest once a week."

Pharaoh thought about it for a moment, then said, "It is true. From now on the Israelite slaves can have one day a week to rest. And, because you Moses are so bright to think of this, you can choose the day."

Moses picked Saturday for the day of rest for the Israelite slaves. And that was the same day that God later gave to the Israelites to be the Sabbath.

[Source: Song of Songs Rabbah 1,28]

# CROSSWORD PUZZLE

1. (down) Amram's wife.
2. (down) Miriam's father.
3. (across) Joseph's father.
4. (across) Moses' sister.
5. (down) Yochebed's son.
6. (across) Ruler of Egypt.
7. (across) What Yochebed used to make a basket.
8. (across) Where the Israelites were made slaves.

# PHARAOH'S MESSAGE

To see what Pharaoh said to his people,
cross out every other letter.

| | | | | | | | | | |
|---|---|---|---|---|---|---|---|---|---|
| T | A | H | B | E | C | I | D | S | E |
| R | L | A | G | E | H | L | J | I | K |
| T | L | E | M | S | N | G | O | R | P |
| O | Q | W | R | S | U | T | V | R | W |
| O | X | N | Y | G | Z | M | W | A | B |
| K | C | E | L | T | N | H | P | E | O |
| M | T | S | U | L | X | A | J | V | Q |
| E | B | S | | | | | | | |

Write the message here:

the isrealites grow strong
make. them slaves.

# COMPLETE THE STORY

Use these words to fill in the blanks.

| REEDS | PRINCE | RIVER | HID | BABY | DAUGHTER | BOY |
|---|---|---|---|---|---|---|

Amram and his wife had a baby__________. Yochebed took__________ and made a basket. She put the basket in the__________ to float. Miriam__________ by the riverside. Pharaoh's__________ came to the river to bathe. When she opened the basket she saw a __________. She took the child to raise as a __________ in Egypt.

# LOOKING FOR UNDERSTANDING

Why did Pharaoh make the Israelites slaves?

___

What was Pharaoh's terrible order?

___

How did Yochebed save her son?

___

What did Miriam do?

___

What did Pharaoh's daughter decide?

___

# MULTIPLE CHOICE

Circle the word that best completes the sentence.

1. The new Pharaoh did not remember all the ___ Joseph had done.
   **good** **jokes** **dreams**
2. Pharaoh thought the Israelites would make ___ against the Egyptians.
   **walls** **statues** **war**
3. Pharaoh ordered that all Israelite baby boys be put in the river and ___.
   **taught to swim** **given a bath** **drowned**
4. Yochebed took reeds from the river and wove them into a little ___.
   **sweater** **purse** **ark**
5. Pharaoh's daughter came to the river to ___.
   **water ski** **fish** **bathe**
6. Miriam offered to find a Hebrew woman to ___ the baby.
   **dress** **kill** **care for**
7. Pharaoh's daughter named the baby ___.
   **Moses** **Joseph** **Amram**
8. Pharaoh's daughter would raise the baby to be a ___.
   **slave** **magician** **prince**

Exodus 2:11-4:18 שְׁמוֹת

*Chapter 17*

# MOSES AND THE BUSH

Moses was brought up in Pharaoh's palace. When he was full grown, he went out to see how the Hebrew slaves made bricks. As he slowly drove his chariot through the valley, he saw a cruel Egyptian taskmaster beating one of the slaves. Moses' heart went out to the slave. He jumped from his chariot and struck the taskmaster with all his might. The Egyptian fell to the ground, dead.

Moses had wanted to do good but he had done evil instead. He was ashamed and afraid. So he hid the body of the dead Egyptian in the sand.

The next day Moses saw two Hebrew slaves fighting, one against the other. This time Moses asked them to stop fighting. But one said, "Will you kill me as you killed the Egyptian?"

Fear froze like ice in Moses' heart. "If these two know that I killed a man," he thought, "soon everyone will know." Then Moses ran away, across the desert. When Pharaoh heard about the murder, he sent soldiers to find Moses and kill him, but Moses was gone.

Moses made his new home in the land of Midian. He built his tent beside the tent of Jethro the Priest and he married Jethro's daughter Zipporah. And, for many years, Moses was happy with his life.

In Egypt, Pharaoh died, and the new Pharaoh made the children of Israel work even harder than before. Their cries of suffering were heard in the heavens high above.

Moses was watching Jethro's sheep near Mount Horeb, the top of which is called Sinai. In the heat of the day Moses spied a flame of fire on the mountain. The fire was in a bush, licking at the branches–but the bush was not burning. Moses was amazed. He said, "I must turn aside and see this great sight."

When God saw that Moses turned aside to see, God called to him out of the bush, saying "Moses, Moses."

And Moses answered, "I am here."

God said, "Come no closer, for this ground is holy. I am the God of your father, the God of Abraham, of Isaac, and of Jacob." Then Moses hid his face for he was afraid to look at God.

God spoke again. "The suffering of the children of Israel is painful to Me. I will take them out of the land of Egypt and bring them to a land flowing with milk and honey, the land of Canaan. You must go to Pharaoh and tell him."

"But I am just a shepherd," Moses said, "Why send me?"

God said, "I will be with you. I will work My wonders until the Egyptians let My people go. Then I will bring you back to this mountain, to this place."



Moses said, "But the Israelites will not follow me."

God said, "Take the rod that is in your hand and throw it to the ground." Moses did, and behold, the rod became a snake. Moses ran away from it.

God said, "Pick up the snake by its tail." And Moses took the snake's tail and, behold, the snake became a rod once again. God said, "The Israelites will see this sign, and they will follow you."

Then Moses said, "But I am a man of few words. How shall I find the right words to speak to Pharaoh?"

God said, "I will put the right words in your mouth. You can also take your brother Aaron who speaks well. I will tell you what to say, and you will tell him. Aaron will speak to the Israelites and to Pharaoh. What I have said will come to pass."

Moses ran to his father-in-law Jethro. And Jethro said, "Go in peace, for God has spoken."

**Each flower is a fine work of art. Yet, when we see a whole field of flowers, we must remind ourselves to "turn aside" to see a single flower.**

WHAT DOES IT MEAN?

## "I must turn aside and see..."

Our sages say: the burning bush was small, yet it was a wonderful thing. Often, the small things in life are very wonderful, but we do not think much about them. We "overlook" them because they are small. When flowers bloom in the springtime, we sometimes look at a pretty field filled with them, but forget to look closely at a single flower to see how beautiful it really is.

In the same way, when people do a little kindness for us, we often forget to thank them. We do not see how wonderful it is when people do even a small thing that helps us.

But Moses "turned aside" to see the bush. He did not pass it by, even though it was a small thing. The Torah says that God was testing Moses, to see if Moses would pay close attention even to the smallest of God's wonders. And Moses did. Then God knew that Moses would pay attention to all the Israelites, from the greatest even to the smallest of them.



WHAT DOES IT TEACH?

## Moses Kills the Taskmaster

It would be wrong to think of Moses as a murderer. The Torah helps us understand what really happened. The story uses the same word to tell what Moses did to the Egyptian taskmaster as it does to tell what the taskmaster was doing to the Hebrew slave. So the Torah is teaching us that the taskmaster was beating the slave in a way that would kill the slave. Moses killed the taskmaster because he saw that it was the only way to save the life of the Hebrew slave.

A LESSON ABOUT THE TORAH

## Whose God is Greater?

A Roman lady was studying Torah with Rabbi Yose. They read the story of the burning bush and the lady laughed. "My god is greater than your god," she said, "and the Torah proves it!"

Rabbi Yose asked how this could be. The Roman lady said, "My god is the snake. Now, look. When your god came to Moses in the bush, Moses only hid his face. But when the rod turned into a snake, Moses ran away from it. So, you see, my god, the snake, is much more powerful."

Rabbi Yose smiled. "That is not the meaning of the story," he explained. "Moses ran from the snake because a snake is only dangerous while you are close to it. A few steps away, you are safe. But our God is everywhere. Where could Moses run? To the heavens? To the bottom of the sea? So Moses hid his face. You can not run away from the One God."

[Source: Ex. R. 3,12]

**Wherever there is water in the middle of the desert, an oasis—a green garden spot—appears. At an oasis like this in the Sinai, Moses watered Jethro's sheep.**

**One legend claims that this raspberry bush in the Sinai mountains grew from the very same burning bush that Moses turned aside to see.**

# WORD SCRAMBLE

The six "S"'s are in the right place, but the other letters are all mixed up. Write the words by putting the letters in the correct order.

**SAKNE** S _ _ _ _

**UIRNNBG UBSH** _ _ _ _ _ _ _   _ _ S _

**ESRALIIETS** _ S _ _ _ _ _ _ _ _

**OMSES** _ _ S _ _

**RBCIKS** _ _ _ _ _ S

**SALSVE** S _ _ _ _ _

# REBUS

God spoke to Moses from the

burning bush. "The suff- 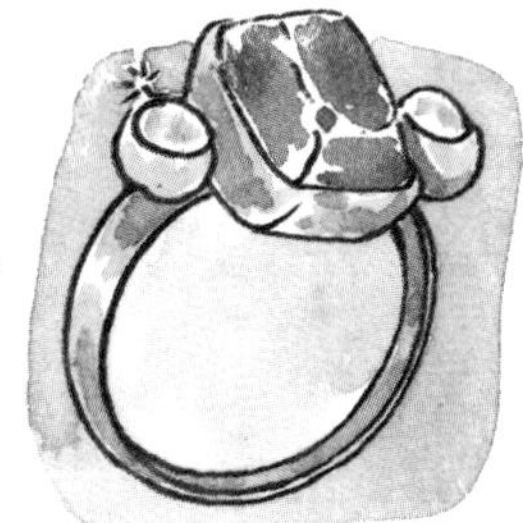

of the Israe-  is painful

 Me.  will take them 

a L- flo-  with  

  the L- of  -an.

 must go Pha- 

tell him  let My 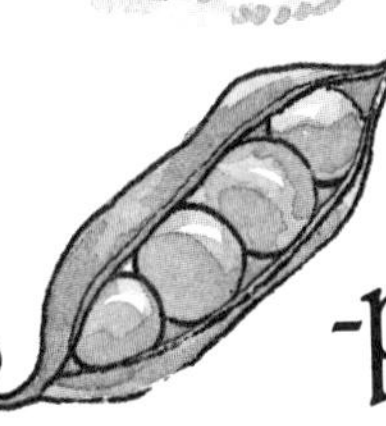 -ple go."

# The Correct Order

All these things happened in the story, but they are not in the right order. Number the sentences in the order that they happened.

_____ God spoke to Moses from a burning bush.

_____ Moses went to see how the Hebrew slaves made bricks.

_____ Moses married Zipporah, the daughter of Jethro the Priest.

_____ Moses ran away, across the desert.

_____ Jethro told Moses to go in peace.

_____ The rod became a snake.

_____ Moses killed the Egyptian taskmaster.

_____ Moses was watching Jethro's sheep near Mount Horeb.



# FEELINGS

How did Moses feel? Use these words to complete the sentences.

HAPPY

AMAZED

ASHAMED

AFRAID

**1**

After Moses killed the Egyptian taskmaster he was

_____________________.

**2**

When Moses married Zipporah he was

_____________________

for many years.

**3**

When Moses saw the burning bush he was

_____________________.

**4**

When God spoke to him from the bush, Moses was

_____________________.

# SMALL BUT WONDERFUL

Sometimes we do not pay close attention to a wonderful thing just because it is small. Think back. What small thing did you overlook? Draw it or write about it.

Exodus 5:1-12:51 שְׁמוֹת

*Chapter 18*

# THE TEN PLAGUES

Moses and his brother Aaron went to Pharaoh, as God commanded them to do. They said to him, "The God of Israel says, 'Let My People go so they may worship Me.'" But Pharaoh answered, "I will not let them go."

The very same day, Pharaoh made the work of the Israelites even harder. He ordered, "Give them no straw to make bricks, but tell them to make the same number of bricks as before."

God said to Moses, "Now you shall see what I will do to Pharaoh. I will force him to let My people go."

Then Aaron threw his rod down before Pharaoh, and the rod became a snake, hissing and slithering on the ground. So Pharaoh called for his wise men and wizards, and they threw down their rods. Each and every rod became a living snake. But the snake of Aaron swallowed up the others. Even at that, Pharaoh refused to listen.

They went outside. As Pharaoh watched, Aaron struck the river with his rod and the water turned into blood. The fish died and the water was poison to drink. But Pharaoh's magicians also turned water into blood. So Pharaoh refused to listen to Aaron and Moses. For seven days the river ran red and full of poison. Blood was God's first plague on Egypt.

Then Aaron stretched out his rod and frogs jumped everywhere. Again, Pharaoh's wizards did the same. Frogs covered the land so that people could not walk without crushing them. Pharaoh said, "Tell your God to kill the frogs and I will let your people go." But when the frogs were gone, Pharaoh changed his mind. The frogs were God's second plague.

Then God sent gnats against the land of Egypt. The bugs filled the air, covering people and animals alike. Gnats were God's third plague. Pharaoh's magicians tried to make gnats, but they could not. They said to Pharaoh, "This is the finger of God." But Pharaoh's heart was hard. He would not listen.

God said, "Tell Pharaoh that I shall send swarms of insects against his land. But this time, only the Egyptians will suffer." The insects were God's fourth plague and only the Egyptians suffered. Pharaoh said, "Free us from this terror, and you may take your people." But when the swarms had passed, Pharaoh again refused to let the Israelites go.

God brought a fifth plague that killed all the Egyptians' cattle, and a sixth plague that caused blisters and boils on the skin of the Egyptian people. Then God sent hail from the sky in a monstrous thunderstorm that covered the whole land. Only where the Israelites lived, hail did not fall. Pharaoh promised to let the Israelites go, but when the hail stopped, he broke his promise once again.

In the eighth plague locusts covered the land of Egypt. Locusts filled every room in every house. They ate the grain and all the trees. Then God sent the ninth plague, three days of darkness so great it could be felt. People could not move even one step. But in the homes of the Hebrews there was light. Pharaoh said to Moses, "Go, and take your people." But Moses said, "You must also give us our cattle." And Pharaoh said, "No."

Then Moses warned Pharaoh, "God will bring one more plague unless you let us go. God will kill the first-born of every Egyptian and every animal in Egypt." Still Pharaoh refused to listen.

Then God said, "Tell the Israelites to make a Passover feast, and to smear the blood of a lamb on their doorposts. The angel of death will see the lamb's blood and will pass over the homes of the Israelites."

And it came to pass at midnight, that God killed the first-born of every household in Egypt. The cries of the Egyptians rose to the heavens, even the cry of Pharaoh, whose first-born son lay dead at his feet.

At last, Pharaoh called Moses and Aaron and said, "Take your people and all their cattle. Take everything and leave Egypt forever. Go and worship your God."

And the people of Israel left the land of Egypt in haste. They did not wait even for the bread dough to rise. They gathered together and followed Moses. By these ten plagues, God brought the children of Israel out of Egypt.

Each year as we sit around the Passover table, we retell the story of Moses and remember how God brought us out of Egypt.

WHAT DOES IT MEAN?

## "This is the finger of God."

Magic is mysterious and wonderful. Pharaoh's magicians were great. They could make it look as if sticks turned into snakes, water turned into blood, and frogs came out of nowhere. But they were just magicians. Their magic was a bag of tricks.



At first, they thought that Moses and Aaron were also magicians. But when the fourth plague began and the gnats were everywhere, they knew that Moses and Aaron were not just playing tricks. This was a magic that they could not do. It was a magic that no magician could do. Only God could make this happen. That is what they meant when they told Pharaoh, "This is the finger of God."

WHAT DOES IT TEACH?

## Miracles

The real miracles of God are already a part of our world. Every one of the ten plagues was something that could happen any time and any place. What made them special was that they happened at exactly the right time and place. They happened just as Moses and Aaron said they would, and in exactly the way that Moses and Aaron said they would. That is what the Torah calls a miracle.

In the same way, miracles happen around us all the time. The earth keeps spinning on just the right path around the sun. The moon keeps spinning on just the right path around the earth. Grass grows. Spring comes. Fall turns into winter. All of these are miracles, too. And, like all the miracles in the Torah, they are a part of our world all the time.

Passover celebrates the miracles of the world. It celebrates the miracle of the plagues, and it celebrates the miracle of spring. And it also celebrates the greatest miracle of all, the miracle of freedom.

These gigantic statues were ordered by the Pharaoh, Rameses II, to be part of his huge temple at Abu Simbel. Perhaps our ancestors helped to build them.

A LESSON ABOUT THE TORAH

## Moses and the Lions

Moses and Aaron went to the palace to see Pharaoh. For other people, coming to the palace was dangerous. Every one of the doors was guarded by a lion. And the lions would kill any strangers who came near their door.

When the lions saw Moses coming, they ran up to him, ready to kill him. But when they smelled him, they remembered him from the time he grew up in the palace. So they licked him and rolled over to let him pet them. They acted like dogs who see their master after a long time.

The Pharaoh must have remembered Moses, too. He did not try to kill Moses or Aaron, even though they came to free the Israelites. After all, Moses was still a prince of Egypt, even though he had run away so many years before.

[Source: Sefer HaYashar]

**The plagues were mostly ordinary things, like the frog in this boy's hands. They became miracles because they came at just the right time. In much the same way, everything in nature is a miracle that God uses to teach us the lessons of the Torah.**

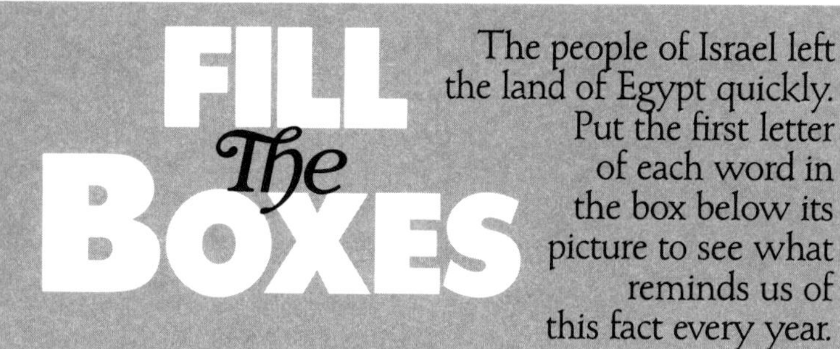


The people of Israel left the land of Egypt quickly. Put the first letter of each word in the box below its picture to see what reminds us of this fact every year.

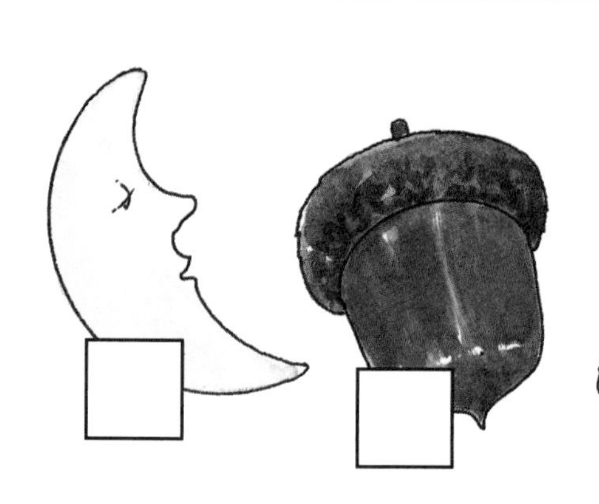

On Passover, we eat________________

## BIBLE DICTIONARY

Draw lines to match the words with what they mean.

- ADAM
- ANGELS
- BIRTHRIGHT
- BLESSING
- COVENANT
- CREATOR
- EDEN
- JEALOUSY
- KEEPER
- KINDNESS

- What Rachel showed Abraham's servant at the well.
- It reminds us of the story of Abraham and Isaac.
- A name that means "a person."
- It happens just in the nick of time.
- A symbol that God will not send another flood.
- The larger share given to the first-born child.
- What we must be for our brothers and sisters.
- Jacob saw many of them on the stairway.
- A kind of pyramid with a stairway.
- The most treasured book of the Jewish people.
- Our teachers in ancient times.
- The garden where Adam and Eve were created.
- A prayer.
- What made Joseph's brothers hate him so.
- How the Israelites learned to love freedom.
- A gift to God.
- God's laws for us.
- A name for God.
- The day of rest that God created.
- An evil place to visit.

- MIRACLE
- RAINBOW
- SACRIFICE
- SAGES
- SHABBAT
- SHOFAR
- SLAVERY
- SODOM
- TORAH
- ZIGGURAT

# MATCHING GAME

Here are the names of important people in the stories you have read. Connect each name to the sentence about that person.

---

- She laughed and called her son "Laughter."
- He was not a good keeper for his brother.
- She gave water to camels.
- He wrestled all night with a stranger.
- The snake talked to her.
- He sold his birthright for food.
- He built a mighty boat.
- He was a slave and then a ruler.
- She and her sister married the same man.
- He was killed by his own brother.
- He was an Egyptian prince.
- He named the animals.
- He argued with God.
- His father took him up a mountain.
- His wife turned to salt.

God made ten terrible things happen in Egypt. Look across and down to find the ten plagues. Circle each one as you find it.

D E A T H O F F I R S T B O R N
A B L D A R H R B L O V O R L F
R L C U I B L O O D L E I S G W
K A K M L D I G N A T S L V P T
N I N S E C T S W R S E S V U Q
E N A D C T K E L O C U S T S R
S L P B M C S Q P A J Z O L H M
S B C A T T L E D I E D I Y A L

Can you write the ten plagues in the correct order below?

1 ____________

2 ____________

3 ____________

4 ____________

5 ____________

6 ____________

7 ____________

8 ____________

9 ____________

10 ____________

# TEST YOURSELF

How much do you remember?
Circle the correct words.

1. God called Abram, "Abraham," and God called Sarai, ______.
   (FOR DINNER) (LAUGHTER) (SARAH)
2. Joseph said to his brothers, "Do not be sad that you sold me. God has sent me ahead to ______.
   (BRING YOU TO EGYPT)
   (BE PHARAOH'S FATHER)
   (SAVE PEOPLE FROM HUNGER)
3. Esau said to Jacob, "I am dying of hunger. What good is my ______ to me?"
   (BIRTHRIGHT) (COAT) (STEW)
4. Yochebed made a ______ for Moses.
   (TENT) (COAT) (BASKET)
5. The stranger said, "Your name is not Jacob any more. It is ______."
   (ISAAC) (ISRAEL) (JOSEPH)
6. God made people in God's ______.
   (TIME) (OVEN) (IMAGE)
7. The brothers took Joseph's coat and dipped it in ______.
   (THE NILE RIVER)
   (GOAT'S BLOOD) (CHOCOLATE)
8. When Sarah died, Abraham bought a ______ in which to bury her.
   (CAVE) (SLAVE) (PYRAMID)
9. Moses said to Pharaoh, "Let My ______ go."
   (CAR) (PEOPLE) (BROTHER)
10. The people of Babel wanted to build a ______ to the sky.
    (PLAYGROUND) (TOWER) (CITY)
11. On the seventh day God created ______.
    (REST) (THE SUN) (SEA MONSTERS)
12. Jacob made a ______ of many colors for Joseph.
    (COAT) (BOAT) (TENT)
13. Cain said, "Am I my brother's ______?"
    (SEEKER) (BARBER) (KEEPER)
14. The ______ is the sign of God's covenant with Noah.
    (RAINBOW) (SUN) STARS)
15. Jacob had a dream. A ______ stood on the earth with its top in the sky.
    (TOWER) (STAIRWAY) (ROCKET)
16. Moses turned aside to look at the ______.
    (BURNING BUSH)
    (MOUNTAINS) (MENU)
17. Abram said to Lot, "We must not argue. We are ______."
    (RICH) (FAMILY) (HAPPY)
18. God said, "I will not destroy Sodom if I find ______ people."
    (EIGHT MIGHTY)
    (TWENTY FUNNY) (TEN GOOD)
19. God said, "It is not good for people to be ______.
    (TOGETHER) (ALONE) (GREEN)
20. The angels said to Lot's family, "Do not ______ back."
    (FIGHT) (LOOK) (RUN)

# AFTERWORD

The children of Israel left Egypt with Moses as their guide. For forty years, they wandered in the wilderness. Then they returned to the Promised Land, the Land of Canaan, and made it the Land of Israel.

Now you have heard the stories and learned the lessons of the beginnings of our people. In the next book, you will see how the Israelites became a great and mighty nation. You will read about kings and prophets, great folk and small. And you will see how the Torah goes on teaching us from generation to generation.

Torah means "teaching." Being Jewish means being ready to learn. That is why the Torah is our greatest treasure.